Applying Institutional Research in Decision Making

John Losak, *Editor*
Miami–Dade Community College

NEW DIRECTIONS FOR COMMUNITY COLLEGES
ARTHUR M. COHEN, *Editor-in-Chief*
FLORENCE B. BRAWER, *Associate Editor*

Number 56, Winter 1986

Paperback sourcebooks in
The Jossey-Bass Higher Education Series

Jossey-Bass Inc., Publishers
San Francisco • London

John Losak (ed.).
Applying Institutional Research in Decision Making.
New Directions for Community Colleges, no. 56.
Volume XIV, number 4.
San Francisco: Jossey-Bass, 1986.

New Directions for Community Colleges
Arthur M. Cohen, *Editor-in-Chief;* Florence B. Brawer, *Associate Editor*

New Directions for Community Colleges (publication number USPS 121-710) is published quarterly by Jossey-Bass Inc., Publishers, in association with the ERIC Clearinghouse for Junior Colleges. *New Directions* is numbered sequentially—please order extra copies by sequential number. The volume and issue numbers above are included for the convenience of libraries. Second class postage paid at San Francisco, California, and at additional mailing offices. POSTMASTER: Send address changes to Jossey-Bass Inc., Publishers, 433 California Street, San Francisco, California 94104.

The material in this publication was prepared pursuant to a contract with the Office of Educational Research and Improvement, U.S. Department of Education. Contractors undertaking such projects under government sponsorship are encouraged to express freely their judgment in professional and technical matters. Prior to publication, the manuscript was submitted to the Center for the Study of Community Colleges for critical review and determination of professional competence. This publication has met such standards. Points of view or opinions, however, do not necessarily represent the official view or opinions of the Center for the Study of Community Colleges or the Office of Educational Research and Improvement.

Editorial correspondence should be sent to the Editor-in-Chief, Arthur M. Cohen, at the ERIC Clearinghouse for Junior Colleges, University of California, Los Angeles, California 90024.

Library of Congress Catalog Card Number 85-644753

International Standard Serial Number ISSN 0194-3081

International Standard Book Number ISBN 1-55542-981-5

Cover art by WILLI BAUM

Manufactured in the United States of America

Office of Educational
Research and Improvement
U.S. Department of Education

Ordering Information

The paperback sourcebooks listed below are published quarterly and can be ordered either by subscription or single-copy.

Subscriptions cost $40.00 per year for institutions, agencies, and libraries. Individuals can subscribe at the special rate of $30.00 per year *if payment is by personal check*. (Note that the full rate of $40.00 applies if payment is by institutional check, even if the subscription is designated for an individual.) Standing orders are accepted.

Single copies are available at $9.95 when payment accompanies order. (California, New Jersey, New York, and Washington, D.C., residents please include appropriate sales tax.) For billed orders, cost per copy is $9.95 plus postage and handling.

Substantial discounts are offered to organizations and individuals wishing to purchase bulk quantities of Jossey-Bass sourcebooks. Please inquire.

Please note that these prices are for the academic year 1986-1987 and are subject to change without notice. Also, some titles may be out of print and therefore not available for sale.

To ensure correct and prompt delivery, all orders must give either the *name of an individual* or an *official purchase order number*. Please submit your order as follows:

Subscriptions: specify series and year subscription is to begin.
Single Copies: specify sourcebook code (such as, CC1) and first two words of title.

Mail orders for United States and Possessions, Latin America, Canada, Japan, Australia, and New Zealand to:
   Jossey-Bass Inc., Publishers
   433 California Street
   San Francisco, California 94104

Mail orders for all other parts of the world to:
   Jossey-Bass Limited
   28 Banner Street
   London EC1Y 8QE

New Directions for Community Colleges Series
Arthur M. Cohen, *Editor-in-Chief*
Florence B. Brawer, *Associate Editor*

CC1   *Toward a Professional Faculty,* Arthur M. Cohen
CC2   *Meeting the Financial Crisis,* John Lombardi
CC3   *Understanding Diverse Students,* Dorothy M. Knoell

CC4	*Updating Occupational Education,* Norman C. Harris
CC5	*Implementing Innovative Instruction,* Roger H. Garrison
CC6	*Coordinating State Systems,* Edmund J. Gleazer, Jr., Roger Yarrington
CC7	*From Class to Mass Learning,* William M. Birenbaum
CC8	*Humanizing Student Services,* Clyde E. Blocker
CC9	*Using Instructional Technology,* George H. Voegel
CC10	*Reforming College Governance,* Richard C. Richardson, Jr.
CC11	*Adjusting to Collective Bargaining,* Richard J. Ernst
CC12	*Merging the Humanities,* Leslie Koltai
CC13	*Changing Managerial Perspectives,* Barry Heermann
CC14	*Reaching Out Through Community Service,* Hope M. Holcomb
CC15	*Enhancing Trustee Effectiveness,* Victoria Dziuba, William Meardy
CC16	*Easing the Transition from Schooling to Work,* Harry F. Silberman, Mark B. Ginsburg
CC17	*Changing Instructional Strategies,* James O. Hammons
CC18	*Assessing Student Academic and Social Progress,* Leonard L. Baird
CC19	*Developing Staff Potential,* Terry O'Banion
CC20	*Improving Relations with the Public,* Louis W. Bender, Benjamin R. Wygal
CC21	*Implementing Community-Based Education,* Ervin L. Harlacher, James F. Gollatscheck
CC22	*Coping with Reduced Resources,* Richard L. Alfred
CC23	*Balancing State and Local Control,* Searle F. Charles
CC24	*Responding to New Missions,* Myron A. Marty
CC25	*Shaping the Curriculum,* Arthur M. Cohen
CC26	*Advancing International Education,* Maxwell C. King, Robert L. Breuder
CC27	*Serving New Populations,* Patricia Ann Walsh
CC28	*Managing in a New Era,* Robert E. Lahti
CC29	*Serving Lifelong Learners,* Barry Heermann, Cheryl Coppeck Enders, Elizabeth Wine
CC30	*Using Part-Time Faculty Effectively,* Michael H. Parsons
CC31	*Teaching the Sciences,* Florence B. Brawer
CC32	*Questioning the Community College Role,* George B. Vaughan
CC33	*Occupational Education Today,* Kathleen F. Arns
CC34	*Women in Community Colleges,* Judith S. Eaton
CC35	*Improving Decision Making,* Mantha Mehallis
CC36	*Marketing the Program,* William A. Keim, Marybelle C. Keim
CC37	*Organization Development: Change Strategies,* James Hammons
CC38	*Institutional Impacts on Campus, Community, and Business Constituencies,* Richard L. Alfred
CC39	*Improving Articulation and Transfer Relationships,* Frederick C. Kintzer
CC40	*General Education in Two-Year Colleges,* B. Lamar Johnson
CC41	*Evaluating Faculty and Staff,* Al Smith
CC42	*Advancing the Liberal Arts,* Stanley F. Turesky
CC43	*Counseling: A Crucial Function for the 1980s,* Alice S. Thurston, William A. Robbins
CC44	*Strategic Management in the Community College,* Gunder A. Myran
CC45	*Designing Programs for Community Groups,* S. V. Martorana, William E. Piland
CC46	*Emerging Roles for Community College Leaders,* Richard L. Alfred, Paul A. Elsner, R. Jan LeCroy, Nancy Armes
CC47	*Microcomputer Applications in Administration and Instruction,* Donald A. Dellow, Lawrence H. Poole

CC48 *Customized Job Training for Business and Industry,* Robert J. Kopecek, Robert G. Clarke
CC49 *Ensuring Effective Governance,* William L. Deegan, James F. Gollattscheck
CC50 *Strengthening Financial Management,* Dale F. Campbell
CC51 *Active Trusteeship for a Changing Era,* Gary Frank Petty
CC52 *Maintaining Institutional Integrity,* Donald E. Puyear, George B. Vaughan
CC53 *Controversies and Decision Making in Difficult Economic Times,* Billie Wright Dziech
CC54 *The Community College and Its Critics,* L. Stephen Zwerling
CC55 *Advances in Instructional Technology,* George H. Voegel

Contents

Editor's Notes 1
John Losak

1. **The Role of Institutional Research in Evaluation of Nontraditional Programs: College Preparatory Analysis at Miami-Dade Community College** 3
Cathy Morris, John Losak
The authors propose an approach to the study of efficacy of remedial programs in the two-year college, with emphasis on process and on the use of incomplete data sets.

2. **The Student Information Questionnaire as a Management Tool for Community College Planning** 13
Judith Moss
This chapter offers an approach to planning for management decisions, which relies heavily on the continual generation of data and emphasizes the dynamic nature of planning.

3. **The Impact of Enrollment Research on Marketing Decision Making and Class Offerings** 27
Gary Rankin
Institutional research data can provide a basis for formative decisions and be used for day-to-day operations during heavy student-enrollment periods.

4. **Strategic Management via Institutional Research** 35
P. Anthony Zeiss
A chief executive officer offers examples of a strategic decision-making process founded on research.

5. **Assessment of Institutional Effectiveness** 49
Kay McCullough Moore
The growing role of institutional research in providing sound assessment and accountability studies is addressed, with respect to accrediting agencies.

6. **Institutional Research and Assessment of the External Environment** 61
Warren H. Groff
This chapter offers a statement of the role of institutional research in assessing changes in environments external to the college and relating these changes to internal decision making and planning.

**7. Campus Leadership: Managing and Marketing Through   75
an Effective Institutional Research Program**
J. Terence Kelly, Ann M. Otto

A view, from administrators who use products of institutional research, of the integral relationships among the offices and staffs of the chief executive, the institutional research department, and the public relations department.

**8. Meeting the Challenge of Change: An Opportunity for Research   85
in the Community College**
Edith H. Carter

The author asks institutional researchers in two-year colleges to focus on identified key areas in the internal and external environments as sources for applied research efforts.

**9. Sources and Information: Institutional Research   99
at the Community College**
Diane Zwemer

This chapter draws upon the ERIC data base to review additional sources of information on institutional research.

Index   111

Editor's Notes

Institutional research in the two-year college in the United States presents a vast array of functions and products, often rendering problematic an answer to the question "What is institutional research in the two-year college?" Offices range from very small, with a director and a part-time secretary, to very large, with five or six research professionals, computer programmers, and several secretaries. Functions vary also and may include completing required documents for state and federal agencies, projecting student enrollment, and conducting impact studies and curriculum efficacy studies.

These multifaceted efforts on the part of institutional researchers across the United States are reflected in the variety of chapters and viewpoints in this volume. The authors were selected for their potential for providing representation across a broad spectrum of geography and functions. All but one of the chapters were written by current or former directors of institutional research; P. Anthony Zeiss (a former institutional research director and now a chief executive officer), J. Terence Kelly, and Ann M. Otto provide perspectives on administrative uses of the products of institutional research.

In the first chapter, Cathy Morris and I provide a heuristic for offices that have components of the ideal package but must present data for decision making. Judith Moss, in Chapter Two, offers the example of institutional research efforts to provide data from an ongoing data source, the Student Information Questionnaire, for planning purposes. In the next chapter, Gary Rankin emphasizes the usefulness of institutional research data in day-to-day decision making during registration. Chapter Four, by P. Anthony Zeiss, gives examples of relationships between strategic decision making and research. Since the importance of outcomes assessment throughout the United States is growing as a component of institutional self-study, Kay McCullough Moore's chapter addresses these new requirements. Warren H. Groff reminds us in Chapter Six of the synergism between the college and the external environment, while J. Terence Kelly and Ann M. Otto, in Chapter Seven, focus on the necessary public-relations uses of institutional research products and, therefore, on the inherent need for close working relationships among the chief executive officer, the public relations staff, and the institutional research staff. In Chapter Eight, Edith H. Carter notes the irony of the fact that funds for institutional research are declining at a time when the need for applied research at the college level has never been greater. Finally, in Chapter

Nine, Diane Zwemer presents an annotated bibliography of selected ERIC documents and journal articles on the community college institutional research function.

John Losak
Editor

John Losak is the dean of institutional research at Miami-Dade Community College, Miami, Florida.

Early, if incomplete, research findings can help direct a strategy of considerable value in evaluation of nontraditional programs.

The Role of Institutional Research in Evaluation of Nontraditional Programs: College Preparatory Analysis at Miami–Dade Community College

Cathy Morris, John Losak

The number of academically underprepared students in postsecondary education has increased in recent years. At the same time, perceptions of declines in academic quality, and losses in college enrollment and funding, have led to increased scrutiny of the relatively high-cost programs for the underprepared (Southern Regional Education Board, 1983). Legislators complain about paying for basic-skills education twice and argue that it properly belongs in the high schools. Boylan (1982) agrees but notes facetiously that multiple payment is not questioned when state contracts are involved or when contractors "pay" for legislators. Maxwell (1979) remarks on the obvious but sometimes overlooked fact that most other college programs are not required to demonstrate their effectiveness. The chemistry teacher is not asked to pre- or posttest, follow students into the next

J. Losak (ed.). *Applying Institutional Research in Decision Making.*
New Directions for Community Colleges, no. 56. San Francisco: Jossey-Bass, Winter 1986.

course, compare grade point averages, or assess long-range outcomes. The next fact that college preparatory ("remedial" or "developmental") programs are scrutinized and held separately accountable indicates that they are seen as nontraditional and perhaps even peripheral to the primary community college mission.

Scrutiny has not necessarily led to systematic research. Kulik, Kulik, and Shwalb (1983) found that of 504 documents related to effects of special programs for high-risk students, only 60 contained sufficient data and/or design parameters to be included in their meta-analysis. The meta-analysis revealed generally positive results for secondary schools and four-year colleges, but the authors noted a relative lack of effectiveness of programs for the high-risk students most often found at community colleges.

For this chapter, our perusal of documents related to community college developmental programs used the same computerized literature-search mechanism (DIALOG) as the meta-analysis study of Kulik, Kulik, and Shwalb. This search revealed thirteen new empirical studies from 1982 onward. Of these, however, four (Cordrey, 1984; Wilson, 1984; Gash, 1983; and Suter, 1983) examined success rates in developmental courses only. The remainder looked at what Boylan (1982) calls secondary outcomes—outcomes for the next course or semester (Johnson, 1985; Joseph, 1984; Bers, 1982); cumulative outcomes after several terms or years (Lutkus, 1985; Borst and Cordrey, 1984; Miller, 1982; Vaden, 1982); or a combination of these (Boggs, 1984: Basonic, 1982). While fairly sophisticated statistics were used in some of these analyses, none evidenced the rigor of random assignment, and only the studies of secondary outcomes attempted comparisons with nondevelopmental students. Lack of empirical data can also be seen in an entire anthology volume devoted to studies of "successful" programs for low-achieving students (Roueche, 1983). Selection criteria for the featured programs are not stated, and most of the chapters simply describe program mechanics, with no evaluation data.

Most authors agree on the need to examine various levels of outcomes in evaluating nontraditional programs. This is especially critical in examining college preparatory instruction, which purports to prepare students for college-level work. Analyses that focus solely on success in college preparatory courses seem attuned to the adult-literacy features of these programs, rather than to their preparatory role. At the other extreme, analyses that focus solely on graduation rates may ignore success in college-level courses for persisters who stop short of degrees.

Faculty and administrator consensus on multiple levels of outcomes was apparent in the results of a Delphi study used to gather opinion on which of several criteria gave evidence of developmental program success in New York State two-year colleges (Fadale and Winter, 1985). The criteria that emerged at the end of the study range from short-range outcomes, such as developmental course completion, to long-range outcomes, such as pass rates in college-level courses and eventual graduation rates. Boylan (1982) calls retention and graduation rates tertiary outcomes and laments that too many studies of underprepared students focus on this level of outcome only. Of the thirteen recent studies reviewed for this chapter, however, only two included longitudinal persistence rates (Lutkus, 1985; Basonic, 1982), and none included graduation data.

The lack of long-range persistence or graduation data is not really surprising. Institutional researchers quite often perceive themselves as lacking resources for long-term studies. Student-tracking systems are usually equated with sophisticated computer programs run on mainframes, rather than with the examination of random samples of transcripts, with data entered into and summarized by a microcomputer. The lead time needed to write sophisticated programs and allow sufficient elapsed time for student follow-up has probably contributed to the lack of tertiary or long-range outcome data in studies of programs for the academically underprepared.

The present chapter provides examples of research effort undertaken at Miami-Dade Community College to analyze the college preparatory program. The analysis began well before a longitudinal data base was available for tracking student outcomes. While an incomplete picture was constructed from the early research, it did provide partial answers and stimulated intense administrative dialogue. On the whole, we shall argue that institutional research, as a process, must proceed with whatever data are at hand, rather than be delayed until accessible mainframe files are completed. Design rigor is maintained when results from quasi-experiments are placed in context. Early, if incomplete, findings can help direct a research strategy of considerable value in the evaluation of nontraditional programs.

Research Using Placement Test Scores

Placement test scores were the first data readily available to us for analysis. While it was not possible to determine which students were enrolling in and completing college preparatory courses, mandatory placement policies made it likely that those below the placement scores in one or more of three basic-skills areas were at least in contact with the college preparatory courses. Initial interest focused on establishing persistence rates for academically underprepared students, as compared to persistence rates for students who entered with no skills deficiencies. In an attempt to anchor data at the extremes, Losak and Morris (1982) contrasted outcomes for full-time students who were tested in fall, 1980, and who passed all three basic-skills components but passed none of the placement tests. The data base was simply a file of students tested in 1980, matched against current enrollment and graduation data. The two-year persistence rate (graduated or still enrolled) for students above the placement score on all three tests was 92 percent, compared to 52 percent for students below the placement score on all three. The persistence rate of students below the placement score on all three tests was primarily accounted for by students who were still enrolled and had not graduated. This was an expected outcome, since completing college preparatory work prior to pursuing college-level courses means that more time is needed to complete degree requirements.

A subsequent study responded to legislative and administrative discussions about the possibility of a clear basic-skills cut point, below which students could not reasonably be expected to succeed, no matter what college preparatory instruction was available (Losak, 1983). Outcomes for students who scored below the twentieth, fifteenth, and tenth percentiles on one or more of the basic-skills placement tests were examined. Once again, the placement testing files were used and matched against enrollment and graduation files. Two additional data elements were included, however, so that more stringent success criteria could be constructed. Cumulative credits earned and grade-point average were both examined, to help ensure that re-enrollment also meant progress. Success was operationally defined as either graduating or earning thirty or more credits, with a grade point average greater than 2.00 (C) after two years. The data demonstrated that there was no clear basic-skills demarcation point below which we could identify students who would not succeed. Success rates for students below all three placement scores at the twentieth, fifteenth, and tenth percentiles were 26 percent, 21 percent, and 23 percent, respectively. While these data were generated from a hastily constructed "patchwork" file, they proved crucial in arguing for maintenance of the open door.

These research findings helped demonstrate success for the academically underprepared, but it is obvious and expected that success rates for such students are lower than success rates for their more academically able counterparts. Efforts to make such students competitive begin with the college preparatory courses at Miami-Dade (as elsewhere) and continue with the normal curriculum interventions provided to all students. The efficacy of the college preparatory experience was not directly addressed in the studies described here, since the early research grouped students on the basis of test scores but did not consider whether students enrolled in and successfully completed their college preparatory courses.

Research Using College Preparatory Course Enrollment

The earliest available data in our files relating enrollment in college preparatory coursework with outcome measures focused on course choices during the first term (Morris, 1982). There were administrative discussions about the benefits of totally immersing students in college preparatory instruction during the first term. The available testing file had a record of courses taken during the first term, and it was a simple matter to match this file to current enrollment and graduation data in order to examine persistence rates. The data showed that highest persistence occurred for students who took both college preparatory and regular college-level courses during the first term. As a result, a total-immersion policy was not enacted.

Persistence rate (combined graduation and re-enrollment rate) was the outcome measure most often used in earlier studies. With the arrival of a statewide sophomore exit exam, however, research began to focus on exit exam passing rates. The college-level academic skills test (CLAST) is the final barrier to graduation from Florida community colleges. The students may not receive an Associate in Arts degree without passing all four subtests of the CLAST. This state restriction made it necessary for the college to monitor student CLAST scores and provided data for institutional research. A retrospective look at college preparatory course enrollment provided a basis for preliminary analyses when longitudinal data were not yet available.

The CLAST was phased in as a statewide graduation requirement, and students were initially required simply to take the exam in order to graduate. Passing scores were not required until the fall of 1984. Preliminary analyses of CLAST success were conducted by application of the passing-score cutoffs to Associate in Arts graduates who took the CLAST before fall of 1984. Losak (1984) examined the files of Associate in Arts graduates who took the CLAST in the fall of 1983. Of these graduates ($N = 1,045$), 35 percent had enrolled in at least one college preparatory course while attending Miami–Dade. Students who had enrolled in even one college preparatory course showed a lower passing rate (58 percent passed all CLAST subtests) than those who had enrolled in none (74 percent passed all CLAST subtests). The available data file made it impossible to determine whether students had successfully completed college preparatory instruction or simply enrolled in courses and entered college-level work before being given satisfactory grades in college preparatory work. One term of enrollment was enough to unlock the system and allow students to proceed to college-level courses. The data did suggest that academically underprepared students might be at a disadvantage when attempting to pass the sophomore exit exam.

A more detailed look at the relationship between college preparatory experience and CLAST success focused on the specific skill areas of reading, writing, and computation. The data base for the fall 1984 CLAST examinees contained detailed information about enrollment in each college preparatory area. This information was related to CLAST skill areas by examining CLAST subtest passing rates for students who were below the cut score in the corresponding area of the entering basic-skills placement test (Belcher, 1985). Outcomes for students who enrolled in the corresponding college preparatory courses were compared with outcomes for students who scored below the entering basic-skills cut scores and who did not enroll in college preparatory classes. Results indicated that there was little difference in CLAST passing rates, in each skill area, between students below the entering basic-skills cut score who took or did not take college preparatory coursework. Belcher concluded that developmental coursework appeared neither to help nor to hinder student performance. Belcher qualified the study results by noting that students who avoided college preparatory coursework were self-selected. Miami–Dade had computer locks in place, and students below the entering basic-skills cut scores had to convince an adviser of their likely success and obtain overrides in order to proceed. A second and continuing caution about the data was that students who took college preparatory coursework may not have successfully completed it.

Research Using a Longitudinal Data Base

The most recent research (Losak and Morris, 1985) was conducted on a long-awaited longitudinal data file. The longitudinal file departed from previous data bases in that it contained placement test scores, as well as data on enrollment in and successful completion of college preparatory work. First-time-in-college students from the fall term of 1982 were chosen for the longitudinal data file because that was the first year of a generally consistent testing and college preparatory placement program. The modal graduation point for students at Miami–Dade, and at most two-year colleges, is the third year; thus, the end of the 1984–85 academic year marked a good opportunity to examine student outcomes.

The study considered outcomes for ten comparative groups with different mixtures of entering basic-skills test performance and college preparatory experience. These groups were composed of students below the placement-test cut scores for up to three areas and, within these groups, it was determined whether students had successfully completed college preparatory work in up to three areas. Students were counted as successfully completing college preparatory work in an area only if they received the S (satisfactory) grade in the highest of several levels of college preparatory courses. The outcome measure used was persistence rate. The study highlighted outcomes for students who successfully completed all college preparatory courses for which they were below the placement scores.

The data indicated that students who successfully completed college preparatory courses in all areas in which they were underprepared had the same persistence rates as students who began with no skills deficiencies. Even students who failed all three portions of the entering basic-skills assessment battery were on a competitive par (46 percent persistence) with those who failed no part of the assessment battery (47 percent persistence).

The data also showed a systematic decrease in persistence rates as fewer required college preparatory courses were completed. For example, the persistence rates for students who were below the placement scores on all three entering tests, and who successfully completed college preparatory work in three, two, one, or no areas, were 46 percent, 37 percent, 23 percent, and 10 percent, respectively.

Since underprepared students must complete college preparatory classes before beginning the normal college-level curriculum, the persistence rate of students below the placement scores on several basic-skills tests was heavily weighted by students who were still enrolled and had not graduated. In order to look at the sophomore exit exam (CLAST) competitiveness of students who successfully remediated some versus all of their basic-skills areas, a new data base of CLAST examinees from the entire 1984–85 academic year was used. This increased the number of students in each comparative group who had reached the point of graduation.

The data showed that students who completed college preparatory work in the areas where they were below placement scores had higher passing rates than students who did not, and the pass rates increased as more college preparatory courses were completed. For example, the CLAST passing rates for students who were below placement scores on all three entering tests, and who successfully completed college preparatory work in no, one, two, or three areas, were 30 percent, 37 percent, 36 percent, and 52 percent, respectively.

The data also showed, however, that students who began with basic-skills deficiencies and successfully completed all their college preparatory work still had lower CLAST passing rates than students who began with no skills deficiencies. The passing rates for students who began college with deficiencies in no, one, two, or three areas, and who successfully remediated all areas, were 95 percent, 84 percent, 64 percent, and 53 percent, respectively. Since an entire curriculum intervenes between college preparatory coursework and the CLAST, a link needs to be made between later course performance and the CLAST. Several existing research studies give clues to why satisfactory remediation still does not place students on a competitive par on the CLAST. More such studies will be undertaken.

Summary and Conclusions

Persistence rate (re-enrollment plus graduation), cumulative credits earned with reasonable grade-point averages, and pass rates on the sophomore exit exam were outcomes examined in the Miami–Dade studies described in this chapter. These measures encompassed several outcome levels, as suggested by evaluators of nontraditional programs in general and college preparatory programs in particular. Further, the studies began with whatever data bases were at hand, even though early results gave only partial answers and had to be qualified and placed in context. It is worth mentioning that analyses of samples of transcripts preceded some of these studies and guided the research direction.

How far wrong was the early picture, compared to the final analysis of the longitudinal data base? In general, persistence rates for students who entered underprepared were lower than for those who did not, but underprepared students who successfully completed college preparatory work showed the same persistence rate as their more academically prepared counterparts. The longitudinal file allowed us to look at successful course-completers apart from students who merely enrolled in college preparatory courses and then entered the college-level curriculum before they were judged by their instructors to have learned basic skills at a satisfactory level. This same logic also helped refine the early picture of CLAST results. The CLAST pass rates of underprepared students who successfully completed college preparatory classes were higher than the CLAST pass rates of underprepared students who did not, yet the early suggestion that the academically underprepared were at a disadvantage on the CLAST was also true. Many of them did not stay in college preparatory courses long enough to be "passed" by their instructors, and this clearly did not bode well for their CLAST success, while those who did complete their college preparatory work still showed lower CLAST passing rates, a finding that led us to examine differential effects of the college-level curriculum.

Thus, the preliminary results were correct but were considerably refined by the more complete data base. Results were shared with administrators and faculty as often as possible, and differences in perspective were accommodated whenever feasible. The college preparatory instructors had felt for some time that students were not showing good judgment in exiting courses before earning passing grades, and results from the final longitudinal data base supported this perception.

These examples demonstrate that "incomplete" institutional research efforts—directed in a phase-in manner and using less than ideal data bases with less than ideal research designs—can nevertheless provide tentative direction for administrative decision making and guide further research efforts.

References

Basonic, N. "The Academic Performance and Persistence Pattern of a Select Group of Developmental Students at Harrisburg Area Community College." Unpublished doctoral dissertation, University of Pennsylvania, 1982. 135 pp. (ED 229 086)

Belcher, M. J. *The Role of Developmental Courses in Improving CLAST Performance.* Miami: Office of Institutional Research, Miami-Dade Community College, 1985. 12 pp. (ED 267 874)

Bers, T. *Follow-Up Study of Students Enrolled in Developmental Communication,*

Fall, 1981. Des Plaines, Ill.: Oakton Community College, 1982. 16 pp. (ED 223 289)

Boggs, G. *The Effect of a Developmental Writing Course on Student Persistence and Achievement: A Research Report*. Oroville, Calif.: Butte College, 1984. 27 pp. (ED 244 687)

Borst, P., and Cordrey, L. *The Skills Prerequisite System at Fullerton College (A Six-Year Investment in People)*. Fullerton, Calif.: North Orange County Community College District, 1984. 10 pp. (ED 255 247)

Boylan, H. "Measuring the Success of Developmental and Remedial Programs." In *Proceedings: Workshop on Improving Developmental/Remedial Education*. Austin: Coordinating Board, Texas College and University System, 1982.

Cordrey, L. *Evaluation of the Skills Prerequisite System at Fullerton College (A Two-Year Follow-Up)*. Fullerton, Calif.: Fullerton College, 1984. 99 pp. (ED 244 663)

Fadale, L., and Winter, G. "Assessing the Effectiveness of Developmental/Remedial Programs in Two Year Colleges." Paper presented at the annual meeting of the American Educational Research Association, Chicago, March 1985. 28 pp. (ED 254 542)

Gash, P. *Remedial Math and Language Arts Study: Effectiveness of Remedial Classes in a Rural Northern California Community College District*. Redding, Calif.: Instructional Research Office, Shasta-Tehama-Trinity Joint Community College District, 1983. 14 pp. (ED 241 091)

Johnson, B. *Success Rate Comparisons for DeKalb Tech Developmental Studies Students*. Clarkston, Ga.: DeKalb Area Vocational-Technical School, 1985. 14 pp. (ED 254 297)

Joseph, N. *Integrated Language Skills: An Approach to Developmental Studies*. Lake City, Fla.: Lake City Community College, 1984. 14 pp. (ED 241 095)

Kulik, C., Kulik, J., and Shwalb, B. "College Programs for High Risk and Disadvantaged Students: A Meta-analysis of Findings." *Review of Educational Research*, 1983, *53* (3), 397–414.

Losak, J. *Relationship Between Comparative Guidance and Placement Scores and Student Success*. Miami: Office of Institutional Research, Miami–Dade Community College, 1983.

Losak, J. *Success on the CLAST for Those Students Who Enter the College Academically Underprepared*. Miami: Office of Institutional Research, Miami–Dade Community College, 1984. 13 pp. (ED 256 449)

Losak, J., and Morris, C. *Retention, Graduation, and Academic Progress as Related to Basic Skills*. Miami: Office of Institutional Research, Miami–Dade Community College, 1982. 29 pp. (ED 226 784)

Losak, J., and Morris, C. *Comparing Treatment Effects for Students Who Successfully Complete College Preparatory Work*. Miami: Office of Institutional Research, Miami–Dade Community College, 1985.

Lutkus, A. *Report to the Board of Higher Education on the Effectiveness of Remedial Programs in New Jersey Public Colleges and Universities. Fall 1982–Spring 1984*. Trenton: New Jersey Basic Skills Council, New Jersey State Department of Higher Education, January 1985.

Maxwell, M. *Improving Student Learning Skills*. San Francisco: Jossey-Bass, 1979.

Miller, C. *Success Comparison of High-Risk Students in Two-Year College Transfer Curricula*. Canton, Ohio: Stark Technical College, 1982. 100 pp. (ED 225 624)

Morris, C. *Retention Rate Related to Choice of First Term Coursework*. Miami: Office of Institutional Research, Miami–Dade Community College, 1982. 15 pp. (ED 256 421)

Roueche, J. E., (ed.). *A New Look at Successful Programs.* New Directions for College Learning Assistance, no. 11. San Francisco: Jossey-Bass, 1983.

Southern Regional Education Board. "Remedial Education in College: The Problem of Underprepared Students." *Issues in Higher Education,* no. 20. Atlanta, Ga.: Southern Regional Education Board, 1983.

Suter, M. "A Comparison of Grades, GPA, and Retention of Developmental Students at Northwest Technical College." Unpublished graduate seminar paper, University of Toledo, 1983. 24 pp. (ED 254 267)

Vaden, S. *Entry Level Skills for Vocational Education, 1981-82. Final Report.* Vineland, N.J.: Cumberland County College, 1982. 53 pp. (ED 241 722)

Wilson, M. *Evaluation of the Solano College Writing Skills Laboratory.* Suisun City, Calif.: Solano Community College, 1984. 30 pp. (ED 254 265)

Cathy Morris is the associate director of institutional research at Miami-Dade Community College in Miami, Florida.

John Losak is the dean of institutional research at Miami-Dade Community College in Miami, Florida.

A questionnaire provides data to support the planning process, not only for administrators and faculty but also for external groups in the local community and statewide.

The Student Information Questionnaire as a Management Tool for Community College Planning

Judith Moss

Decisions are constantly made in community colleges, for the same reason as in any other organization. There is constant change. Resources, facilities, funding, faculty, and students affect the status quo. Community college enrollments are extremely sensitive to external factors, particularly population changes, employment opportunities, and public perceptions of the value of education.

The need to react to these constant changes is the strongest argument for community college planning. Planning is considered to be a continual process of learning about all facets of the institution. This process orientation of planning negates the often-heard criticism that one cannot plan because of the dynamic nature of community college activities. It allows for an identified course of action but recognizes flexibility. With knowledge comes understanding, and then comes the ability to make quick decisions based on accumulated experience. These gut-level decisions reflect a situation where alternatives have been considered even in advance of need. Planning emphasizes that information is needed to respond to specific questions, as well as to provide background for questions not specifically posed. The more complete the understanding of all aspects of the institution, the better the management of change. The current emphasis in the San Francisco Community College District is on planning as a process.

With the thirst for knowledge to support the planning process come the questions of what knowledge and what data are to be collected, presented, and used. Institutional researchers must determine whether operational data can be used or special surveys are required.

As indeed they are to any institution, these basic questions about research data are fundamental to community colleges, particularly because of the limited resources available. The major emphasis of community colleges is teaching rather than research and is reflected in the orientations and interests of staff. It is also reflected in the funds available for research, whether for research offices or for faculty researchers.

The San Francisco Community College District has long recognized that data and analysis are needed for management and planning. This chapter discusses how the San Francisco Community College District addressed its need for information about one segment, the students, who are indeed both the raw material and the end product of the educational process. It will describe the student information questionnaire (SIQ), which is both the process and the data collected every other year since 1972 in the San Francisco Community College District, and will include examples of varied uses of the SIQ. For readers who may consider replicating it or adopting features of it, a brief discussion on methodology is included.

The San Francisco Community College District

The San Francisco Community College District, created in 1971, includes two operating divisions, each under the administration of a president. These two divisions are the City College of San Francisco and the Community College Centers division. City College enrolls about 7,000 full-time students and 16,000 part-time students, all in credit classes. A broad curriculum is offered, providing opportunities for students to complete requirements for Associate in Arts and Associate in Science degrees or to transfer to four-year colleges or universities, as well as to one-year semi-professional programs or to courses needed for entry-level jobs or job upgrading.

The Community College Centers division offers noncredit courses administered through seven administrative centers. Each center offers specific program specialties, as well as serving different neighborhoods in the city. About 32,000 students participate at any one time in such diverse offerings as occupational and apprentice training, adult basic education, and special programs for seniors and handicapped or disadvantaged persons. Also offered are community service classes, for which fees are charged, and contract education, in which a class may be tailored for a specific employer at a charge to cover all expenses. Most students attend only part-time, but those in certain vocational programs or high school and ESL courses may be full-time students prior to entering the job stream or attending City College.

Need for Student Data

Community colleges by and large carry out well their essential task of teaching students, but today that is not enough. Education is in the spotlight, for myriad reasons; it must be accountable to citizens for the limited resources available and to students for the time and effort they invest. In California, eyes are on the community colleges because of the changing nature of the community college student, in terms of both demography and educational objectives. Community college education is largely tax supported; tuition is not yet charged, but there is a nominal fee of five dollars per unit, or fifty dollars for six or more units per semester. In 1985 the state legislature created the Commission for the Review of the Master Plan for Higher Education, whose first responsibility was a community college reassessment study, slated for release in the spring of 1986. It will be followed by legislative consideration, probably leading to significant regulation and funding changes.

The commission study emphasized the need for facts relevant to what is being taught, to whom, and with what success, in order to substantiate policy recommendations. Program planning is one of the key areas in which management skills must be exercised, using fact rather than opinion, and recognizing the need for educational variety in accord with the mission statement. Key questions concern the nature of the students served and their educational objectives. It is not only our faculty and administration who ask these questions; these questions are asked, in general terms, by the legislature, and then specific subsets of these questions are asked by each legislator, depending on his or her specific interest or constituency. Thus, data on students are needed for both internal and statewide planning, for responses to myriad questions, and even for defense against critics. The status quo is hardly ever a valid option, and certainly not today, with changes occurring in the social, economic, and ethnic characteristics of students. We need data to reach conclusions and to substantiate subsequent actions.

For many years, City College has maintained data by discipline on student attendance and weekly student contact hours. Faculty full-time equivalents have also been summarized, so that one measure of efficiency can be calculated, but effectiveness measures have been missing, as these numbers do not relate to students but only to numbers of students. It was recognized that facts on student demographics in each discipline were needed. Another area of defined data need is that of student outcome, or measures of student success. (Information on other components of an educational institution—namely, staff, facilities, and funding—are also important but are beyond the scope of this chapter.) Background perspectives on the future of San Francisco and on societal trends, together with statements on the district's missions and goals, were published in 1984 as an educational "master plan."

Student data had been available to meet current operational needs, but not planning needs. Operational data were limited to a few basic demographic elements, such as age, sex, and ethnicity. Use of operational data for planning purposes approaches optimum cost-effectiveness, but how many additional data elements should be collected and stored on an ongoing basis? At the other extreme, special-purpose data may be collected as a one-time project to meet specific study purposes.

An issue compounding the question of data collection for analytic purposes in the community colleges is the concern, or perhaps even fear, of the uses to which the data may be put. Will demonstrated or projected declines in programs have negative consequences for involved staff? Will different student populations require different teaching methods? Fear of the uses of data has been recognized as a critical area for staff development activities.

At City College, an application form collects basic demographic data about the student, which are then transferred to a computer data base. Then, an on-line registration system processes the student's class assignments into a class file. At the Community College Centers, with their open and continuous enrollment policies, students enroll with no formal registration process. Thus, student demographic information has not been readily available from this enrollment process. Only in the last year has information from enrollment cards been transferred to the computer system to begin an automated student data base; it is expected to become increasingly useful for analytic and planning purposes. Nevertheless, it does not, nor is it expected to, include all the desired information on students and on their expectations that is needed for planning. Thus, an alternative source of data has been available in the Community College Center division since 1972 and at City College since 1976.

The Student Information Questionnaire (SIQ)

Upon the creation of the new district in 1971, the need for information on the noncredit student body was immediately apparent. What started out as a simple questionnaire, to replace a show of hands in each class and meet state-mandated data requirements, became an ongoing system to provide information about the Community College Centers division's very diversified student body. It would be many years before the centers would be automated, even to a minimal extent. This need was recognized as an opportunity to coordinate and consolidate bits and pieces of information about the student body into an ongoing system. Thus, in 1972, the student information questionnaire (SIQ) was born.

The SIQ is administered to all students every other year to ask them questions about themselves and their educational goals. In the centers, students' responses are combined with information about each class they attend. Next, a variety of computer runs summarizes all student responses and program data for any parameter selected either from the questionnaire or from the class identification. Thus, demographics can be compared for students who have different educational objectives or are in different program categories. Most of the 1984 questionnaire is shown as Exhibit 1, and a section of the computer-prepared report is shown as Exhibit 2. The computer runs are the heart and value of the SIQ. The uses range from serving as a reference to answering simple requests to influencing policy makers at the state and local levels.

Uses of the SIQ

Although the SIQ was initiated in 1972 to meet state-mandated data requirements, it was recognized that a more important purpose was to provide an ongoing picture of students. No explicit statement was made at that time as to how the data would be used, other than in general terms of policy analysis. Now its actual use has far exceeded the most optimistic expectations. Frequently, when a needed answer might be found in the operational data base, we find that it is more readily available in the SIQ. A recent survey of field administrators cited their many applications of SIQ information, emphasizing the local and diversified uses, some of which the district was unaware of. Following is a brief discussion of some of the ways in which the SIQ has helped in the management of the district.

Transportation and Parking Facilities. One of the major student concerns, and therefore an administrative concern is transportation to and from classes. A simple, single-purpose survey of a student sample had identified the magnitude of the problem but could not identify the students in need. It was readily apparent that the SIQ would be a more useful device, because a full set of student demographics would be available for any desired stratification. A question was therefore included in the SIQ on the usual mode of transportation to class. City College could be reached both by the bus system and by the Bay Area Rapid Transit, and limited parking space was available. Age, sex, ethnicity, income, and occupation of students driving to class could be contrasted with characteristics of students using public transit. The SIQ also showed the differences between day and evening students. As in all transit systems, fares are reviewed

Exhibit 1. Student Information Questionnaire

*The Community College Center I am now attending is ....
  1. Alemany   3. John Adams   5.   7. Chinatown/North Beach   9. Downtown Center
  2. Galileo   4. Mission   6. John O'Connell   8. Skills Center   0. Other

The information summarized from this survey will be used for planning purposes to enable us to meet the educational program needs of the adults in the community. Therefore, you will receive this questionnaire in each class that you attend. Even though you may be asked to complete it more than once, please help us by answering all questions in each class that you attend, and return the completed form to your teacher.

ZIP CODE of My Home Address is (write five numbers on lines at right) .... ___ ___ ___ ___ ___

FOR EACH QUESTION, CIRCLE THE NUMBER OF ONLY *ONE* ANSWER THAT BEST DESCRIBES YOU, AND WRITE THAT NUMBER IN THE CORRECT SPACE IN THE COLUMN AT THE RIGHT.

A. Sex .... A. ____
  1. male   2. female

B. Age (at last birthday) .... B. ____
  1. under 18   3. 20   5. 25 - 34   7. 45 - 54   9. 60 - 64
  2. 18 - 19   4. 21 - 24   6. 35 - 44   8. 55 - 59   0. 65 or older

C. Race or ethnic background .... C. ____
  1. Alas. Nat./Amer. Ind.   3. White (not Hispanic)   5. Chinese   7. Japanese   9. Other Asian/Pac. Islander
  2. Black (not Hispanic)   4. Hispanic/Latino/Chicano   6. Filipino   8. S.E. Asian   0. Other (specify)_____

D. Citizenship status .... D. ____
  1. U.S. citizen - native born   4. refugee-parolee - S.E. Asia   8. visitor visa
  2. U.S. citizen - naturalized   5. refugee-parolee - U.S.S.R.   9. student visa (1 - 20)
  3. permanent resident (green card)   6. refugee-parolee - Central, S. America   0. other visa (specify)_____
    7. refugee-parolee - other

E. My primary language at home is (select only one) .... E. ____
  1. Spanish   4. Korean   7. Mandarin
  2. Cantonese   5. Vietnamese   8. Japanese
  3. Pilipino/Tagalog   6. English   9. Other (specify)_____

F. I am a U.S. military veteran .... F. ____
  1. prior to Vietnam   2. Vietnam era   3. post-Vietnam   4. no U.S. military service

G. I usually get to class mainly by .... G. ____
  1. car, I drive   3. bus/streetcar   5. bicycle   7. motorcycle
  2. car as passenger   4. BART   6. walking   8. other

H. Number of years of school I have completed .... H. ____
  1. 6 or less   3. 9 or 10   5. 13 or 14   7. 17 or more
  2. 7 or 8   4. 11 or 12   6. 15 or 16

I. In the *United States*, the highest diploma, certificate or degree I have received is .... I. ____
  1. education not in the U.S.   4. high school   7. community college (AA or AS)
  2. did not complete elementary school   5. G.E.D. or Proficiency Certificate   8. college or university (BA or BS)
  3. elementary school   6. occupational certificate   9. post graduate (MA, PhD, MD . . .)

J. I found out about this class from .... J. ____
  1. friends   3. District schedule sent to my home   5. inquiry at school   7. newspaper   9. other publicity
  2. teachers or counselors   4. this Center's notice sent to my home   6. catalog   8. radio or T.V.

K. My *main* reason for taking this course is to .... K. ____
  1. work for my high school diploma   6. determine my ability for a new occupation
  2. complete my college prerequisites   7. reenter job market
  3. prepare for entry-level job   8. learn or improve my English
  4. get a better job in my present occupational field   9. learn specific life skills
  5. change to a new occupation   0. broaden my background

L. The number of hours per week I attend Community College Centers classes is .... L. ____
  1. 1 - 2   3. 5 - 6   5. 10 - 11   7. 16 - 17   9. 24 - 30
  2. 3 - 4   4. 7 - 9   6. 12 - 15   8. 18 - 23   0. 31 or more

M. The last time I took a class offered by the Community College District was .... M. ____
  1. Summer 1984   2. Spring 1984   3. Fall 1983   4. two or more years ago   5. never

N. I work for .... N. ____
  1. Federal government   3. City government   5. self-employed   7. other
  2. State government   4. private business   6. nonprofit agency   8. not employed now

O. My *main* occupation now is .... O. ____
  1. full-time employed, 30 hours or more   4. looking for work   7. volunteer work
  2. regular part-time work   5. full-time homemaker   8. full-time student
  3. occasional part-time work   6. retired   9. other

P. The *one* student service I expect to use most is .... P. ____
  1. career counseling and guidance   4. student financial aid   7. child care
  2. educational and program planning   5. gay/lesbian counseling   8. other
  3. job placement assistance   6. personal problem counseling   9. none

Exhibit 2. Computer-Generated Report

```
SIQ-07      01/10/85              STUDENT INFORMATION QUESTIONNAIRE CENTERS DIVISION - FALL 1984
                                        SAN FRANCISCO COMMUNITY COLLEGE DISTRICT
                                  EVERY COMMUNITY COLLEGE CENTER BY SPECIAL PROGRAM
```

	HI-SCHOOL REGULAR		G.E.D. PROGRAM		SENIORS		HANDICAPPED		OCC-PREP		OCC-SUPL		APPRENT	
QUESTIONS	NO.	PCT	NO.	PCT	NO.	PCT	NO.	PCT	NO.	PCT	NO.	PCT	NO.	PCT
O PRESENT OCCUPATION														
1 WORK FULL-TIME	164	22.1	131	17.9	82	3.8	127	7.9	1040	23.2	682	25.1	572	73.3
2 WORK REGULAR P.T.	88	11.8	67	9.2	59	2.8	91	5.7	511	11.4	160	5.9	25	3.
3 WORK OCCAS'N P.T.	35	4.7	23	3.1	24	1.1	21	1.3	244	5.4	74	2.7	8	1.0
4 SEEKING WORK	149	20.1	189	25.9	37	1.7	135	8.4	953	21.3	306	11.2	61	
5 HOMEMAKER F.T.	27	3.6	37	5.1	186	8.7	34	2.1	155	3.5	99	3.6	2	
6 RETIRED	33	4.4	38	5.2	1420	66.7	130	8.1	69	1.5	851	31.3	77	9.
7 VOLUNTEER WORK	15	2.0	18	2.5	90	4.2	50	3.1	82	1.8	141	5.2	8	1.0
8 FULL-TIME STUDENT	188	25.3	176	24.1	34	1.6	306	19.1	1234	27.5	250	9.2	15	1.9
9 OTHER	44	5.9	52	7.1	198	9.3	706	44.1	195	4.3	158	5.8	14	
TOTAL	743	100.0*	731	100.0*	2130	100.0*	1600	100.0*	4483	100.0*	2721	100.0*	782	100
P STUDENT SERVICE														
1 CAREER GUIDANCE	110	14.9	83	11.4	12	.6	109	6.9	666	15.1	181	6.8	75	9.9
2 ED PROGRAM PLANNG	121	16.4	192	26.4	53	2.6	108	6.8	783	17.7	211	7.9	118	1
3 JOB PLACEMENT	65	8.8	129	17.8	14	.7	127	8.0	1178	26.6	381	14.2	139	18
4 FINANCIAL AID	39	5.3	75	10.3	21	1.0	23	1.4	505	11.4	130	4.9	16	2.
5 GAY,LESBIAN COUNS			4	.6	3	.1	8	.5	15	.3	7	.3	4	.5
6 PERSONAL PROBLEMS	5	.7	17	2.3	143	7.0	77	4.9	36	.8	52	1.9	5	.7
7 CHILD CARE	29	3.9	23	3.2	17	.8	19	1.2	111	2.5	53	2.0	3	
8 OTHER	69	9.3	52	7.2	484	23.8	318	20.0	261	5.9	267	10.0	70	
9 NONE	302	40.8	151	20.8	1287	63.3	798	50.3	869	19.6	1398	52.2	329	43.
TOTAL	740	100.0*	726	100.0*	2034	100.0*	1587	100.0*	4424	100.0*	2680	100.0*	759	100.0
Q MAIN PROBLEM														
1 READING SKI		4.0	75	.3	6			1.0	86	.9	39			3.0
2 WRITING SK				.7	4					3.1	17			.9

periodically. The debate raged in City Hall on feasibility of special fares for students. In response to a request from a member of the Board of Supervisors, information from the SIQ was provided to show in what neighborhoods the students lived, what their income levels were, and how they currently came to classes. This demonstrated reliance on public transit, particularly among low-income students.

More recently, the SIQ was used to respond to a major public issue: adequacy of parking at City College, and alternatives. On campus, as in most urban environments, student (and faculty) parking is at a premium; a large lot on city-owned land is used for parking on a long-term but temporary basis. The city is now considering other uses of that land parcel. It was important to advise the city administration not only on use of the parking lot but also on the demographics and residence areas of students driving to class. Members of the Board of Supervisors would then know their City College constituencies and how their decisions might affect them.

In these instances, the ultimate decision was out of the hands of the district administration. However, the SIQ enabled the administration to present a coherent set of facts, with only the added effort of searching the data resources. Then a quick analysis could be made, leading to a definitive policy statement. In arguing before public bodies, it is crucial to have facts to back up policy statements; frequently there is not time, and certainly there are not funds available, for special projects to respond to each pending decision.

Location of Facilities. In the centers division, classes are offered in seven administrative centers throughout the city and at additional off-site locations. Residents of one community petitioned the governing board for a major administrative center to be located in their neighborhood. Using the SIQ data by neighborhoods, the administration was able to demonstrate that residents of the specified area attended classes in the different centers more because of subject matter than geography. Further, current students were compared with the population demographics (using census data) to determine whether that neighborhood was underserved, as compared to others. It was demonstrated to the board's satisfaction not only that the cost of a new facility in that area was not warranted but also that it would be unlikely to attract additional students. What was demonstrated was that better public-information activities were needed to advise the community of all the available programs.

In another instance, almost the reverse of the above, the SIQ was used to demonstrate the need for expanded facilities in one center and then to describe the student body that might use that new facility, if provided. The feasibility of a new site in the target area was proved. A combined public service and educational facility was built as a mitigating measure, imposed as a result of a mandated environmental impact report. The new facility opened in the fall of 1986, and the most recent SIQ is being used to refine the program offerings and discuss with faculty the ethnic-cultural background of probable students. Another center used geographical and program data to determine the optimum location for evening classes and then rented classroom space accordingly.

In these instances, the SIQ alone, or with census data, was used for needs assessment, without special surveys. Information from the SIQ served to help clarify administrative decisions. It is not possible to say whether or where a new facility might have been arranged had the SIQ not been available, but it gave insight into the problems under discussion. Decision makers had the facts they needed to respond to their constituents and to special-interest groups.

Student Services. Although instruction is its key function, the San Francisco Community College District recognizes the need for a variety of student services, so that students can better avail themselves of classroom activities. The centers division offers a broad program to a clientele much more diversified than the more traditional community college student body. The administration needed a body of information to describe students who felt the need for a variety of student services and to compare them both with those who had expressed no need and with those who actually received such services. The SIQ provided such information, enabling better planning and coordination of these services. A side benefit of the SIQ was to reinforce in students' minds that such services were available to them in the centers division.

Program Planning and Evaluation. One of the most critical management areas today is ensuring that the programs offered meet student and societal needs. A very comprehensive program-review activity has been undertaken in the San Francisco Community College District, in which teams of faculty and administrators review in depth every program on a three-year cycle. One of the important elements of that review is an understanding of who the students are and what their objectives are. Organizing the data into program classifications affords such analysis. The SIQ for the centers provides a classification of courses, both by discipline and by groupings into state-mandated areas for adult education. Thus, a comprehensive analysis of students for each program is readily available and is especially useful in discussion of statewide issues. It can be demonstrated, for example, that large proportions of students in some courses, which might be considered avocational, had very clear and immediate vocational objectives.

As comparable data have been available since the first SIQ in 1972, the changes in the student body in each program can be analyzed. Modifications in programs can be offered to meet the observed changes, and faculty can employ teaching methodologies more appropriate to the changing student clientele. Without the SIQ, we would have reacted only to changes in the number of students, rather than changes in the character of students.

The SIQ implemented at City College since 1976 did not include programmatic data, a deficiency that was noted and has now become very obvious, both in program review and in preparing for hearings of the commission on the master plan. We need, for example, insight into the students in remedial and below-university-level math and English courses. Although some data are available in the student registration data base, they are not so comprehensive as the SIQ data. The minimal analysis that we were able to make from the computer data base has convinced staff of the necessity for a complete SIQ at City College, which would include programmatic data; it is to be included in the 1986 SIQ design. The analysis of student characteristics and objectives is the most important aspect of the SIQ and through the years has been most helpful in influencing legislation.

Unexpected Benefits. The first SIQ itself brought a very unexpected and significant benefit to the district. The SIQ results were validated against known parameters, a standard procedure in survey work. When the results could not be validated in regard to one set of data elements of the SIQ compared to operational data, the survey was suspect. Further analysis indicated, however, that the survey was correct and operational procedures were faulty, leading to a significant underclaim of state apportionment funds to which the district was entitled; of course, the attendance reporting system was redesigned. For that one year alone, it was worth about $485,000 in district revenues. As often happens, research provides benefits in most unexpected ways. Over the years, the analysis of the SIQ has led to other operational improvements and cost savings, but its main value is in improved education.

SIQ Methodolgy

The SIQ is a summary of information about students supplied by each student. It is combined with data about courses taken, and then it is presented in tabular form for analysis. This section will outline briefly the method adopted and the reasons for the design. Any reader wanting more detailed information may contact the author.

Questionnaire Design. Because of the nature of the informal registration process for the center division, it was quickly determined that we should use a specially designed questionnaire, rather than building on the enrollment process. The questionnaire had to be short and simple, both to be understood by the diverse student body and not to take much time away from instruction.

A list of potential questions, each with up to ten multiple-choice responses, was developed. Multiple-choice response was selected, rather than freeform completion, not only because of ease of coding and subsequent machine processing but also because wording of potential responses clarified the intent of the questions, thus reducing their wordiness. Questions were suggested by a divisional administrator knowledgeable about the operations of the division and respected by faculty and staff. Questions and appropriate responses were discussed with other division administrators and tested in several classes before their adoption.

The determination of the questions and possible responses to be included is one of the most important aspects of an SIQ design and it should involve large numbers of faculty and other potential users to ensure both meaningful and useful responses. Broad involvement is necessary in sifting out the questions so that only the most useful are included. This has become increasingly important, as the SIQ is now used by a much broader spectrum of faculty and administrators.

The questionnaire was designed on a single page, first for ease of response and second for ease of key entry. The initial questionnaire in 1972 included seventeen questions. The 1984 questionnaire included twenty-one questions, also within the one-page design, which was possible because of more creative use of type fonts. Over the years, a few questions were dropped, and new ones were added to meet specific needs; wording and response choices were modified as experience dictated. However, care was given to maintaining consistency, in order to study trends useful for projections.

By limiting the number of questions, we knew not only that all recommended questions could not be included but also that a single question might result only in an approximation of the desired information; however, an approximation with consistency was still valuable. For example, to ensure the validity of income data from a single question is difficult, even impossible. Nevertheless, for the SIQ, just one question, adapted from the census, was used to ask the student's household income level; further, *household* was not defined. This provided a gross and consistent measure of student income and was an adequate indicator for analytical purposes. As the SIQ is adapted for use in other institutions, questions of specific importance to that institution must be included.

Questionnaire Administration. Since the survey data were to be secured by a questionnaire to be completed by students, the next design consideration was where and when. Mailing to the student's home was too expensive; even more important, the uncontrolled and unknown segment of nonresponse would be expected to yield unreliable results, especially for analysis by small subgroups. Administering the questionnaire in centers division classrooms offered the opportunity to explain the survey purpose, so that students would agree to complete the survey instrument with reliability. Equally important, it provided the opportunity to include programmatic data by incorporating class parameters.

Sampling was quickly ruled out because data were needed for small subgroups of students. Because of the many disciplines offered and the many site locations around the city, a stratified sample of classes to provide large enough subgroups for each program on such data elements as ethnicity and residence area was not feasible, and to administer the questionnaire in each class to only some of the students would create severe administrative problems. Therefore, a 100 percent response rate was requested, and better than 90 percent was achieved, with no obvious pattern of omissions. The questionnaires are anonymous, with the expectation that students will be more open and honest. Students have cooperated, with only a few exceptions.

The instructors returned the completed questionnaires to the center divisional SIQ coordinator, together with an identifying cover sheet. The returned batches were checked against the master control list of all classes, to ensure that all class batches were received and that the number of responses was reasonable in comparison to the number of class enrollees.

Editing and Coding. The divisional SIQ coordinator was then responsible for a team of student work-study aides who coded and edited as necessary. The editing assured that the coding was done correctly or completed when there was an omission. The editing staff then reviewed each student response sheet to catch obvious errors—for example, if a student wrote in "twenty-nine" for age, rather than the proper response-code number. The editing staff clarified legibility, such that a key-entry operator could quickly enter the data into machine-readable format. Editing is the major cost item, but as more and more reliance is placed on the SIQ analysis, it is an essential step. Proper orientation prior to SIQ administration will improve accuracy and reduce the editing task.

Key Entry. The questionnaire format was designed with key entry in mind. The operator needs only to scan the right margin for entries, rather than searching the page. Before that design, careful consideration was given to optical scanning, but costs and technical problems argued against it. To expedite the process, the use of an external key-punching service may be beneficial, because key entry is a large-volume, one-time job. The keying was done onto tape, according to a protocol established by the data processing department. The appropriate class identification codes were automatically added to the response record for each SIQ in the class batch, such that a unit record was completed for each student response.

Computer Processing. The computer program was initially written to specifications in 1972 and modified slightly over the years, primarily to meet hardware changes and to refine the output format so that it could be published directly. The reports show the number of valid responses and the percentage distribution for each SIQ question, spread by any of the course descriptors or SIQ characteristics desired, or by residence areas. Exhibit 2 shows one page of the special program run.

SIQ Report. The final step in the formal SIQ process is the analysis and publication of the data. In 1984, the published volume included analysis of the 1984 data as well as trend analyses since 1972, together with implications of the findings. It also included copies of the basic computer runs, so that the document also serves as a reference resource useful to respond to a large variety of questions.

Costs. In considering whether to replicate this study, the reader certainly will want to consider costs. The out-of-pocket costs included the paper for the SIQ questionnaire and the report itself, the key-entry services for the questionnaire responses, and salaries for the student editor-coders. Sufficient lead time was allowed for printing and for computer time to be scheduled, without incremental cost.

The significant costs are in terms of time rather than dollars. Planning time and meetings to involve users in the design should not be underestimated. Control of the distribution and collection of responses must be carefully considered. Then, staff time must be allowed for data analysis and report preparation. The cost, of course, will not necessarily result in savings; the value is in the ability to offer the education to which our students are entitled.

Time Line. The time line is actually about one year for a complete cycle. The SIQ is administered in the fall of alternate years. During the preceding spring, the questionnaire is discussed, and final agreement is reached on the specific questions to be included that year. During the summer, the questionnaire is produced. At faculty planning meetings in the fall, the SIQ process is described. Students complete it in the fall. Editing begins soon thereafter, with key-entry in early December. Computer time is scheduled during the winter recess, when fewer students will need access to the system. In January or February, summary reports are made available, and the finished publication is released in the spring.

Conclusion

The SIQ is used not only internally by administrators and faculty but also by many external groups, ranging from community groups to state legislative and staff committees. The report, particularly the summary and trend analyses, can be useful for overall insight into our students. A reader may browse through summary runs for items of specific interest or search more deeply for responses to problem areas. The research office staff is available to discuss interpretations or make special analyses. It is now difficult to conceive of the district facing the complex future without this tool.

Judith Moss is interim vice chancellor for the San Francisco Community College District, San Francisco, California.

Formative research allows for a managed decision-making process in day-to-day activities during enrollment.

The Impact of Enrollment Research on Marketing Decision Making and Class Offerings

Gary Rankin

Marketing in colleges and universities has become a common practice over the past ten years (Kotler and Fox, 1985). Long-range marketing plans have become an integral part of the college's strategic planning process. Although marketing is an effective component of the planning process, little has been written describing how marketing activities or enrollment data can be managed and evaluated on a day-to-day basis. The question arises of how decisions regarding target-group priorities and class offerings can be made during instead of after enrollment. The focus of this chapter is to describe how one college has managed enrollment decisions with respect to marketing priorities and class offerings on a day-to-day basis. A description is presented of how formative research on enrollment patterns and class offerings is collected and evaluated at Oklahoma City Community College.

Review of the Literature

Most enrollment/marketing research appears to be summative. After enrollment, data are collected and analyzed and decisions are made for the next enrollment period. Several research studies have supported the importance of marketing research in the decision-making process. Bryant (1982) indicates that effective marketing and enrollment-management techniques should be an institutional priority. He discusses the need for effective data collection and appropriate decision making in order to maintain desired enrollment levels. Rice (1979) reports the need to incorporate institutional research directly into the college decision-making process. He describes the important role that computers and management information systems can play in this process. An "informal action research model" is described by Losak and Morris (1985) in their discussion of how decision makers can use data in their deliberations. Mehallis (1981) describes several studies that have influenced decision making. Her review mentions several essays that focus on the importance of accurate and timely information for effective decision making.

Review of the literature reveals that most research studies related to decision making and marketing were conducted between enrollment periods rather than during enrollment. One study deals with the cancellation of classes (Jones, 1976); it, too, however, offers a summative look at the impact on students. There is virtually no formative research that deals with marketing efforts and decision making with respect to class offerings.

Table 1. Categories for Daily Enrollment Report[a]
Used to Manage Marketing Activities,
by New and Returning Student and by Sex

Original Type of Admission	*Race/Ethnic Group*
First time	American Indian
High school	Hispanic
Transfer	Black
Special	White
Other	
Receiving Benefits	*Class Attendance*
Veterans Assistance	Morning
Financial Aids	Afternoon
Vocational Rehabilitation	Night
	Arranged
Students 55 and Over	*High School Graduates*
Noncredit to credit students	1985 Graduates (First Time)
Noncredit enrollment	1984 Graduates (First Time)
	1985 Graduates (Transfer)
	1984 Graduates (Transfer)

[a] Reported by headcount and credit hours.

Background

Oklahoma City Community College is a comprehensive two-year community college. Since the inception of the college, the systems approach to management, instruction, and evaluation has been used. The college is in a suburb of Oklahoma City and attracts students from the greater metropolitan area. The mean age of the student population is over 30; 85 percent of the students attend part-time, 65 percent attend evening classes, and over 90 percent work full-time. The college's academic calendar has seven entry points. To accommodate both student planning and multiple enrollments, the enrollment period for each entry point is at least three months long. Since 1976, an on-line student data base has been used to enroll students and provide daily information on student characteristics and class sizes. As the college's marketing plan was developed and expanded, the data-based management system was also expanded. Table 1 indicates the basic data available in the daily enrollment report that is provided to the institutional officer responsible for marketing. As can be seen, data are available by recruitment target groups and are broken down by sex and by new and returning students. In addition to enrollment data on target populations, data are also available on enrollment patterns by academic division (institutes) and class section.

Table 2 shows the data available on class offerings. The information in this report is used to determine whether additional sections of a course should be opened or whether a course should be cancelled because of low enrollment. Enrollment information is available by academic institute, program, and course. In addition, data are presented that allow comparisons among morning, afternoon, night, and arranged sections. This information is produced weekly for the seven entries offered by the college.

Data Elements

Daily enrollment information, as summarized in Table 1, is available for each target group and is broken down by new and returning student categories. Table 2 reflects data that are available by class section. This information shows both the requested section size and the maximum size available and indicates enrollment at weekly intervals, starting four weeks before classes begin and ending two weeks after classes begin.

Decision Making in Marketing

Although the marketing plan is developed to generate recruitment, retention, and promotional activities on a strategically planned basis, the formative data available from the daily enrollment reports allow ongoing modification of plans. As the current year's figures are compared with

Table 2. Categories for Weekly Enrollment Report Used to Manage Class Offerings

Morning Section Totals	Requested Class Size
Afternoon Section Totals	Class Size 4 Weeks Prior
Night Section Totals	Class Size 3 Weeks Prior
Arranged Section Totals	Class Size 2 Weeks Prior
	Class Size 1 Week Prior
Totals by Institute	Class Size 0 Weeks Prior
Totals by Course	Class Size 1 Week After
Totals by Section	Class Size 2 Weeks After
Totals with Advanced Standing	

previous years' figures, "soft spots" can be identified, and rapid decisions can be made, as required. Recruitment is the responsibility of the Student Relations Office, retention is the responsibility of the dean of instruction, and promotion is the responsibility of the Public Information Office, but daily enrollment data are reported to all college managers. Marketing objectives are written into each college manager's contract; thus appropriate daily responses to enrollment data can be made by each manager of the college.

Decision Making in Class Offerings

A key component of the college's marketing plan is the faculty. The faculty's role is defined through institutional marketing plans. There are six institutes: the institutes of business and management, allied health, social science and human services, electronic information systems and mathematics, science and manufacturing technology, and communications and the arts. Each January, during faculty orientation week, institute marketing plans are evaluated and developed. The institute marketing plans focus on retention but also identify an enrollment target, targeted populations, and activities for recruitment and promotion. As the start of classes draws near, all institutes and program areas evaluate the daily and weekly information for their respective courses.

Table 3 shows the weekly academic enrollment summary used by the academic managers. Each manager can compare enrollment trends with the previous year's weekly totals, the previous year's final, and the current year's target. If the data indicate that extreme variances exist with the projected target, then appropriate activities are implemented or intensified. Four weeks before classes begin, reactive plans can be initiated. With all courses, the "go/no go" decision is made the week before the beginning of classes. Data used for this decision-making process are the criteria set for acceptable enrollment (fifteen paid enrollments), the number

Table 3. Weekly Academic Enrollment Summary
for Managing Class Offerings

Institute	Target	-4	-3	Week -2	-1	0	c1	c2
C & A								
B & M								
S & MT								
SS & HS								
AH								
EIS & M								
CM								
Total								
% of Last Year								
% of Last Year's Final								
% of Target								

of paid enrollments, the history of late enrollments, the course's importance for graduation requirements, and the number of activity sections.

Evaluation

The use of the enrollment data, made available through the on-line student and enrollment data base at Oklahoma City Community College, has been evaluated as very helpful in the decision-making process. The formative evaluation has provided data important in the consideration of program and target-population goals that are not being met. Summative data have allowed modifications in strategic planning, which have affected annual marketing plans.

Three major components of the data-collection system have been identified for modification through the evaluation process. The first one concerns the relationship between the start of classes and dates set for cancellation of student enrollment because of failure to pay tuition and fees. Currently, sections with low enrollment may be cancelled the week before classes begin. This is also the week student enrollments are cancelled for nonpayment of tuition and fees. In several cases, decisions were made to run sections on the basis of current enrollment figures, but after student cancellations, actual class enrollments fell below the specified criterion of fifteen students. The recommendation is that enrollment data, by section, be available on both gross enrollment and paid enrollment.

The other two areas where additional data are needed concern transfer students and returning students. An emerging target population is the reverse-transfer student. Currently, the data provided by the management information system does not differentiate the transfer student's last date of enrollment in an institution of higher education. Thus, if activities are planned for students transferring from colleges or universities within the last two or three years, and if the majority of transfer students entering Oklahoma City Community College have been out of college for more than five years, these activities are not effective. Thus, it is recommended that data on new students who have attended other institutions be separated by year of last attendance at a college or university. Additional data are also needed on returning students. Here, as with data on transfer students, the source of the data affects recruitment efforts. The nature of the Oklahoma City Community College promotes the presence of "stopouts"—students who stop attending for two or three terms and then return. Summative research reveals that only 30 percent of the students enrolled in any given term are new students; thus, 70 percent of the students enrolled are "stopouts" or continuing students. These students become a major issue in the evaluation of recruitment and retention activities, with respect to the length of absence of the 70 percent who return. The recommendation is that the returning-student data be broken down by length of "stopout" periods.

Summary

In addition to summative research, it is important to conduct formative research to influence decision making. Evaluation of the research methodology used at Oklahoma City Community College has revealed that summative research for marketing activities and class offerings provides for long-range strategic planning, while formative research allows for a managed decision-making process in day-to-day activities during enrollment. The outcome is a systemic approach to the marketing and the decision making that are related to class offerings.

References

Bryant, P. S. "Enrollment Management—A Priority." In P. S. Bryant and J. A. Johnson (eds.), *Advancing the Two-Year College.* New Directions for Institutional Advancement, no. 15. San Francisco: Jossey-Bass, 1982.

Jones, R. F. *A Study of the Impact of Cancelling Classes.* Rockville, Md.: Office of Institutional Research, Montgomery College, 1976.

Kotler, P., and Fox, K. *Strategic Marketing for Educational Institutions.* Englewood Cliffs, N.J.: Prentice-Hall, 1985.

Losak, J., and Morris, C. "Integrating Research into Decision Making: Providing Examples for an Informal Action Research Model." *Community/Junior College Quarterly of Research and Practice,* 1985, *9* (1), 55-63.

Mehallis, M. V. (ed.). *Improving Decision Making.* New Directions for Community Colleges, no. 35. San Francisco: Jossey-Bass, 1981.

Rice, G. "Institutional Research in the Two-Year College: Messiah or Leper?" In R. G. Cope (ed.), *Professional Development for Institutional Research.* New Directions for Institutional Research, no. 23. San Francisco: Jossey-Bass, 1979.

Gary Rankin is vice-president for student development at Oklahoma City Community College in Oklahoma City, Oklahoma.

Executive officers must develop an entrepreneurlike and research-based approach to the management and leadership of their institutions.

Strategic Management via Institutional Research

P. Anthony Zeiss

As the demand for community colleges to diversify services to multiple publics increases, the need for effective decision making by top management has become critical. Indeed, the strategic management techniques utilized by successful entrepreneurs in the private sector offer valuable direction for educational administrators. Myran (1983) succinctly states the issue by referring to "the academic management revolution." It has been generally accepted that top-level educational personnel are administrators, rather than managers. The distinction between the two is clearly defined. Administrators are primarily involved with myopic, internal decisions, which mostly affect the day-to-day activities of an institution. Managers, however, are externally and internally focused, with a special mission for shaping the institution's present and future life. The success or failure of any community college today depends primarily on the ability of its top-level leadership to make valid, efficient, and effective decisions, decisions based on pertinent and reliable research data.

       Fisher (1984) frequently emphasizes the importance of research in the decision-making process for presidents. Indeed, the entire book is designed to provide research-based, validated behaviors that make for successful presidencies. Keller (1983) purports that it is time for all of America's higher education institutions to begin viewing themselves as part of the mainstream of this country, rather than as separate and sacrosanct. At this time, he says, "unless new patterns of leadership become more prevalent, U.S. higher education will have an even more tearing time in the coming decade than many expect." Presidents simply must begin to participate in planning for the future of their institutions, rather than simply trying to anger the fewest people.

By their very nature, community colleges have accepted the comprehensive role of providing a plethora of learning opportunities and services to a broad array of publics through open-access policies (Anderson, 1985). This is not to say that community colleges are attempting to be all things to all people, or that the impact of the nation's community colleges has been diluted by the wide diversity of its services and publics. Rather, this diversity of specific purposes provides the real strength and the very essence of a community college's utility. An institution's ability to anticipate, identify, and respond to the emerging needs and interests of its students is essential to its success. In this respect, community colleges from the beginning have successfully emulated the entrepreneurs of our free-enterprise system. The challenge before all community college presidents and other top-level managers is to control this tradition of responsiveness in the face of ever-increasing student needs, job restructuring on a national scale, and more complex constituencies.

A traditional, almost natural, response to complex issues is to simplify them. The National Commission on Excellence in Education (1983) report stirred the emotions and intellects of millions of educational and governmental leaders across the United States. State after state soon began to adopt relatively simple solutions, including mandatory adoption of higher college-entrance standards and the elimination of remedial courses at four-year institutions. The call for teacher competency testing, for example, appears logical from a surface perspective; however, testing teachers' skills will scarcely ensure effective teaching (Hawley, 1985). The results of such legislated actions remain to be realized and evaluated, of course. However, it is relatively safe to state that no amount of legislation, financing, or self-imposed regulations will seriously alter the excellence of our colleges unless the basic units of our learning system, the teachers, buy into the newly regulated processes and unless top-level managers learn to make critical decisions through well-researched and institutionally strategic processes. Certainly the teachers and support staff should be involved in all major decisions affecting instruction, curriculum, and delivery. The salient point, however, is that top-level community college managers must be more than administrators, more than caretakers of their institutions. Presidents and chancellors of community colleges and community college systems must be prepared to make accurate, timely, and wise decisions for the current and future well-being of their colleges. If these top-level managers fail to make the right strategic decisions, history demonstrates that our legislatures, and rightly so, will be making the decisions for us. Today's college manager must be wise enough to take advantage of the available external and internal research services at his or her institution. This simple process will allow the manager to make a decision and implement an action plan based on valid data, once those data have been analyzed and the alternatives have been thoroughly reviewed. The age of research-based decision making at the community college has arrived, and we can ill afford to ignore this opportunity.

Of the 1,221 public community colleges in this country, it is estimated that only 60 percent have designated full-time institutional research persons (American Association of Community and Junior Colleges, 1985), yet as a relatively new system of higher education we have a tremendous need to understand what we are doing well, where we can improve, and what we should be anticipating in the future. Too many colleges, it appears, have elected simply to be reactive institutions, without the benefit of research-based support data, which could foster a more anticipatory and active mode of operation. Further, a school and its leaders must be active in the decision-making process regarding institutional planning and the historical position of the institution. Keller (1983) summarizes the importance of strategic thinking: "To think strategically is to look intensely at contemporary history and your institution's position in it and work out a planning process that actively confronts the historical movement, overcomes it, gets on top of it, or seizes the opportunities latent in it." There are also institutions that have research departments, but whose presidents fail to recognize the worth of the data or the potential value of these departments from a strategic perspective. Certainly the door swings in both directions. Research directors have a responsibility to seek out the research needs of institutions, but presidents and other managers should not fail to take advantage of their research departments when involved in the decision-making process.

A Strategic Decision-Making Process

With the case being made for community college managers to develop and utilize a strategic decision-making process centering on valid research, a basic process model should be described. This model is in no manner all-inclusive, but it does include the essential ingredients, according to Rumelt (1979), and it has served one institution well (Myran, 1983).

Essentially, any decision-making process, to be effective, must involve the basic mission of the institution, its goal, and its objectives. Further, an effective decision-making process will seek input from its internal and external publics in an ever-changing environment. The following process model can be very effective if used consistently:

1. Determine need;

2. Gather pertinent and valid data;
3. List and evaluate alternatives (data analysis);
4. Select best alternative(s) or opportunities;
5. Develop and delegate action plan; and
6. Monitor and evaluate results.

This model is dynamic when research (steps 2 and 6) is at the core of the activity. Indeed, the evaluation of an action may identify new needs, problems, or opportunities. The degree of participation involved in the process is entirely arbitrary, of course, and a lengthy discussion of the merits of participatory versus autocratic methods in the decision-making process is not necessary here. It should be sufficient to mention that a broader knowledge base in making decisions is often more effective than a narrow scope of knowledge and perspectives. There is some speculation that a school-based decision-making process relates positively to a school's effectiveness (Duke, 1984). It should be noted, however, that efficiency also drops as larger numbers of participants are involved. Active participation of appropriate personnel should certainly occur during steps 1, 3, and 4.

A Case Study

To illustrate the model process, as described, the following case study involving Pueblo Community College and this writer, as president of that institution, is presented. It should be noted that throughout this three-year activity, a bona fide research department did not always exist at the institution. However, the research participants felt ownership of this activity, and the data gathered proved to be reliable.

The basic mission of Pueblo Community College is to provide effective job training and personal improvement. In the fall of 1982, the school had only recently evolved, as a result of a legislative decision to split the two-year vocational component from the University of Southern Colorado. The school had been so involved with the political and social aspects of this change that it had not yet taken an introspective look at itself. As a consequence, a two-month instructional needs assessment was conducted in the fall of 1982. The data gathered were not totally comprehensive; however, the process did involve every element of the campus, and the results clearly indicated some critical need areas. Each of these critical areas—curriculum update, equipment update, classroom space, inefficient student advising and admissions procedures, and high student attrition—then became subjects for additional specific research, with separately prescribed but oftentimes overlapping action plans. This total diagnostic-prescriptive activity continued three years later. Because of the dynamic nature of the decision-making process, as described, it will continue indefinitely.

One of the most critical areas discovered was that the college, in the fall of 1982, was experiencing 41.7 percent attrition from students leaving

the school between the first and second semesters. Student retention quickly became a concern. As a first step, the managers compiled a list of "influencing factors" to be investigated. These influencing factors included:
- Comfort levels of the campus
- Campus marketing efforts
- Availability of remediation courses
- School admissions process
- Advising and counseling procedures
- Institutional image
- Career assessment services
- Academic standards
- Student orientation procedures
- Social, cultural, and economic factors
- Instructor attitudes and awareness of the problem
- Readability levels of textbooks
- Effects of probation and suspension
- Academic and demographic profiles of students
- Dropout trend data
- Class attendance.

Aside from the internal research efforts related to these identified influencing factors, a review of recent literature on community college student retention was undertaken. Levitz (1984) stated that a high-quality campus is a key to retention and that students must have successful and rewarding experiences in programs and with campus services. Wide research substantiates that the more students perceive they are being successful, the more likely they are to persist (Levitz, 1984; Reed, 1981). Further, the first six weeks of a student's experience on campus are most critical in determining whether he or she stays or leaves (Levitz, 1984), and according to Keller (1983), improved educational programs and student services must come to the forefront, and competition for students should be an institutional goal.

Fortunately, a great deal of research has been accomplished in the area of retention. Study after study discusses the need for better student advising and for recognizing that ethnic and cultural factors affect student persistence, that freshman orientation classes contribute to student retention, and that remedial and career assessment programs markedly improve student retention (Coker and others, 1985; Losak and Morris, 1983; Jones, 1984; Rounds, 1984; Bray, 1984; Cohen, 1984). The literature review substantiated the "influencing factors" and assisted in broadening the knowledge base of the college's decision makers. A summary of the literature was reviewed with the institution's entire faculty and staff, in an effort to increase institutional awareness of the problem and to foster acceptance of the forthcoming actions and activities.

After much discussion and thought by the college's administrators, a three-phase plan of action was developed to meet the alternative opportunities related to the problem. The three phases of the action plan included curriculum renewal, development of assessment and remediation sources, and image improvement. Phases one and two were completed in 1983 and 1984, respectively, and phase three will be completed by the end of the 1985-86 academic year. Throughout this decision-making process, the available research plus the learned perceptions and experiences of the administrative staff were thoroughly considered. The action plans were well communicated, and positive faculty participation was relatively easy to accomplish, given the broad recognition of the problem.

Phase One: Curriculum Renewal

It was clear from the instructional needs assessment that a standardized curriculum format, which included skill-based performance requirements, was needed at the institution. Pueblo Community College at this time was totally technical in nature except for general education courses. The action plan for this phase included the development of a standard competency-based curriculum format, which measured student performance; the development of a student profile; and the measurement of readability levels of all textbooks and occupation-specific work manuals.

The standardized curriculum format was developed according to the premise that it should be based on industry-validated competencies, should be performance-oriented, and should have high utility. Further, the curriculum format had to be adaptable to academic as well as occupational courses. The final format included a syllabus, a set of unit plans, and set of lesson plans, all color-coded for utility and all based on measurable objectives. The institution provided group and individualized training sessions for all faculty, and the entire program offerings of the school were converted to this format and teaching method in one year. Instructors simply wrote their curricula as they taught them each semester.

The development process was in many ways as important as the final product. Instructional expertise among many of the faculty rose greatly. Further, the utility of the curriculum improved 100 percent. Substitutes and new teachers knew what to teach, and students understood what was expected of them. The choices for student success increased greatly once this critical area, the very heart of the instructional process, was improved.

Concurrent with curriculum development, an accurate student profile was developed. In 1982, this profile revealed that the average student's age was thirty, that ethnicity mirrored the school's service-area population, and that the average reading, computation, and communication levels hovered around the 7.5 grade level. It is needless to mention that these data validated suspicions that the school should begin mandatory basic-skills assessments and that it should significantly increase its remedial offerings. These data also revealed the much-suspected need to conduct readability studies on each program's textbooks. Thanks to the research, the institution now knew precisely what types of students it was serving, and top-level management began to utilize this information in all its future student-related decisions.

Readability studies were conducted in every instructional department and by every instructor. Each instructor was trained to evaluate his or her course textbooks and respective industry operational manuals. The texts were evaluated in order to develop some sound internal choices, and the occupational manuals were evaluated in order to establish an exit readability level for graduates by program. Again, the process of evaluating the readability levels was as valuable as the product. The instructors' awareness levels in this respect increased significantly. Many textbooks were evaluated at the sixteenth-grade level, yet the students were reading at an average level of the seventh grade. It was little wonder that the school had high student attrition. This activity culminated with the publishing of an institutional directory, which listed the readability levels of each text by program, the operational manuals' readability levels by program or occupation, and the average reading, computation, and communication levels needed to function in each occupational program offered by the college. This publication was distributed to all faculty, with instructions to share the information with students and to take corrective curricular action as necessary. It is significant that all the described activities and subsequent policies were research-based.

Phase Two: Development of Assessment and Remediation Services

In 1984, management at Pueblo Community College set a clear course for the expansion of remediation services and for the development of a comprehensive assessment center. The first activity again involved research. A faculty committee researched scores of basic-skills assessment tests, to be used for a soon-to-be established mandatory assessment battery for all students. After much review and pilot testing, the school elected to adopt one commercially designed test for reading skills. The liberal arts faculty then designed and validated assessment instruments for mathematics and communications. The data processing department designed and validated a basic assessment instrument for computer awareness. The chief academic officer then established the policy that all new students, with rare exceptions, would take the basic-skills assessment before developing their course schedules. Further, any deficiencies discovered would require enrollment in appropriate remediation courses. Even then, students would have to improve to satisfactory levels before enrolling in college-level English or mathematics courses. All faculty and administrative personnel were mobilized to ensure that the new mandatory assessment policy would function effectively. The remediation classes increased threefold during the first semester in which the new policy was implemented.

The institutional research director also conducted a historical search of nonreturning students and the relationship to class attendance. This study revealed a direct relationship between class attendance and achievement. It further substantiated the premise that students who are not achieving will have high potential to drop out of college. The analysis of this data resulted in an institutional policy to require a mandatory "administrative drop" from any college-credit class where a student was absent for 20 percent of the clock hours. There was uniform acceptance of this new policy among the faculty and very little turbulence among the students.

The final piece of this phase of the three-year activity involved the development of one of Colorado's most comprehensive career assessment centers. Again, a review of relevant literature indicated that effective career counseling eliminated most student program changes. Top-level management secured special grants from several state and federal sources to develop the career assessment center. After the hiring of a professional staff, a significant amount of research was conducted regarding the actual assessment instruments, systems, and procedures to be utilized. The staff ultimately developed an extremely comprehensive diagnostic-prescriptive assessment center, which offered a "menu" of assessment opportunities to students. This menu provided myriad testing alternatives—to include interest, aptitude, occupation-specific hand and finger dexterity, sensory skills, perceptual skills, physical capabilities, and so on—which ranged in duration from one to twelve hours. This career assessment center quickly became an integral part of the entire community. Virtually every job training agency contracted with the school to assess clients. This side benefit of student recruitment was a much-welcomed surprise. Two thousand people were tested through the career assessment center in its first eight months of operation. All nondeclared majors (students) are automatically referred to the career asessment center.

Subsequent development research in this area revealed needs for easily understood career information, increased job-preparation skills training, and hands-on environmental career experience. Much of the research consisted of a simple tabulation of interests and requests from the assessment center's clients and from suggestions by college faculty and administrators. Nonetheless, the decisions to create a career information section in the center, to require mandatory job-preparation training for all graduates, and to develop a hands-on laboratory-based evaluation carrel for each of the school's training were based on reliable data. Developing the career information section and implementing the job-preparation training were relatively simple and inexpensive. To provide hands-on occupationally specific evaluations within the laboratories of the school's twenty-seven programs was complex and expensive. Fortunately, the college obtained the necessary federal funds to develop the additional assessment activity. This activity proved to be most important, not in relation to the student's performance but in the value of an environmental experience. The initial career assessment battery, for instance, may suggest that the student will do well in the welding field. The laboratory-based evaluations, however, may reveal that the student has a fear of fire or is allergic to burning welding-rod smoke. This environmental experience has been most valuable to students who were still undecided on occupational training areas after the initial assessment. The instructor's evaluation of this hands-on experience is also valuable, and the opportunity to talk with an instructor seemed to be of much benefit to both parties.

Phase Three: Image Improvement

During the fall of 1985, the college president initiated yet another research project for the purpose of image improvement. Recent literature supports the theory that an institution's internal image and the free flow of communication among staff and students is directly related to student attrition (Harrower and others, 1980). A simple survey, asking (1) what the respondent liked most about the college and (2) what single improvement was most needed, was received from 64 faculty and staff and 260 students. The results clearly indicated that a large majority of students were very satisfied with the school and its services. However, several areas were identified as being in need of improvement. The faculty-staff survey results were more complex and more difficult to interpret. Nonetheless, it was clear that institutional loyalty and commitment were widespread. The greatest needs cited by this population included a better flow of communication to the administration and better instructional equipment and facilities.

Some specific activities took place as a result of the internal image study. The president began a periodic "faculty-staff coffee" in order to improve communication. "Student coffees" were already in place, and a nationally renowned institutional marketing consultant was hired to provide a campuswide in-service workshop. The school was closed for half a day, and all employees attended the workshop. Key administrators and faculty worked with the consultant for a full day. It is safe to say that the awareness level of marketing among the college's employees rose considerably. Further, the essential belief that all employees are working toward the same goal of service to students became predominant. Both the internal and external images of the institution improved because of this activity. A third major conclusion, drawn largely from the student survey responses, was that there was an immediate need to improve the school's admissions and intake procedures and a need to improve the school's student advising procedures.

Again, the need and justification for utilizing institutional research as a method for institutional decision making and for establishing an institution's direction was established. Pueblo Community College now had valid data from which to develop and implement meaningful institutional improvement activities.

Concurrently with the image study, the research arm of the institution conducted a targeted research project and developed the first comprehensive marketing plan. An institutional marketing committee, representative of all service areas of the school, was formed to review the marketing plan and to determine applicable action strategies to improve marketing. Marketing, in this sense, involved the total environment of the college, not just student recruitment. Again, solid research data were used as the basis for institutional action and direction.

Finally, since data supplied by the National Center for Student Retention indicated that nearly 85 percent of all first-time student contacts with a college came by telephone, Pueblo Community College again reacted. This research finding was discussed with various college personnel, and it was concluded that the statistic was likely to be valid for the college. In consequence, the president arranged for two "telephone etiquette" training sessions and required attendance by all secretaries, receptionists, and work-study students who answered telephones.

Results of Research-Based Activities at Pueblo Community College

Although it is too early to determine the final influences of all the described institutional student retention activities, it is clear that Pueblo Community College now has a basis for marketing and a high awareness of student attrition and is being operated from a research-based model for strategic decision making. It is interesting that there was very little negative student and faculty reaction throughout the development and implementation of all the described activities. Indeed, the results for student retention and faculty involvement were most positive. As of January 1986, Pueblo Community College has the highest percentage enrollment increase among all colleges and universities in Colorado for the previous two years. The college was continuing to enjoy the top position in student job placement for all higher education institutions in the state, and student attrition from semester to semester had dropped, from 41.7 percent in the fall of 1982 to 30.4 percent in January of 1986. Clearly, the case for top-level management to utilize its research capabilities for decision making and for setting institutional directions is valid, viable, and practical.

The Case for Research

If we in the community college sector of American higher education truly believe in the essential role our institutions play in this nation's life, we must regard our services as directly related to national concerns. These concerns—for social justice, economic growth, civic and cultural enrichment, and national security—must be addressed in our services to students (Boyer, 1985). The case for utilizing research data to decrease student attrition is valid and practical. An extended use of this same research-based method for relating our student services to the greater national concern is equally valid and practical. Indeed, there is reason to believe that educators and private citizens who serve on various national commissions to study higher education recognize the tremendous value of research in the decision-making process. In 1984, the study group on the conditions of excellence in American higher education proposed that "the Department of Education solicit advice from a broad cross section of the research community and other informed parties to address the quality of current educational data, to suggest the kinds of data that ought to be maintained, to consider the processes by which such data are collected in many agencies, and to recommend reporting capacities that would be useful to the educational community at large" (National Institute of Education, 1984, p. 21). Further, a 1985 Carnegie Foundation special report recommends that the importance of higher education research should be reconsidered and that higher education should be at the forefront in research if the United States is to remain globally competitive (Newman, 1985).

Evidence is also found at the state and local levels that the importance of using research data for decision making is clearly recognized. One of the major goals of the Colorado Consortium of Two-Year Community/Junior Colleges presented to the Colorado Commission of Higher Education is "to maintain research efforts throughout this educational improvement project to assist in decision making" (Keller and others, 1985). Specifically, this task group, representing all fifteen Colorado community colleges, stated that research activities, including institutional assessments, formal longitudinal studies, and statewide assessments, were essential for the success of the proposed educational improvement strategies in Colorado.

Research and the Learning Process

Perhaps the greatest opportunity and challenge for managing community colleges strategically via institutional research lies in research and the learning process. Eurich (1985) states that "higher education has done little to learn about teaching and learning." Eurich, in a familiar manner, suggests that the major stride in understanding the learning process and in adopting more effective and efficient teaching techniques may well come from the private sector, rather than from higher education: It appears that higher education, unlike the private corporate world, does not seek to improve its own performance by systematic investment in innovative research and development. Corporate leaders, however, fully realize the importance of the value of significant research and development. It is becoming increasingly apparent that knowledge has become people's most important resource. The need for revitalization and regrouping of our education and training systems, especially with regard to the current trend for technological change and displaced workers, is greatly needed. If we, as collective community college leaders, hope to help our country maintain an advantageous world position, and if we individually hope to maintain a positive institutional posture, we must recognize the importance of the learning process and become committed to the appropriate research in this process. Whether this vital activity is eventually conducted institutionally or via a national forum is of little consequence now. Top-level administrators of community colleges will do well to utilize the strategic decision-making process, via institutional research, in the immediate investigation of whom they are serving, how students learn best, and how the schools can best be of service.

Concluding Remarks

This chapter has been a brief attempt to demonstrate the need and a workable method for community college managers to utilize institutional research in the strategic decision-making process. From researching this topic and by reflecting on relevant personal experience, this author offers three basic tenets for presidents and other executive officers of community colleges who hope to lead their institutions successfully:
1. They must become leaders and managers, not simply administrators.
2. They must develop an entrepreneurlike approach to the management and leadership of their institutions.
3. They must develop and utilize a research-based process for evaluating and making critical decisions.

The future seldom evolves in the way we would like, unless we have elected to take some responsibility in shaping it. The future of community colleges, collectively and individually, rests primarily with top-level administrators and depends on their ability to seize opportunities and make wise management decisions. The proper guidance and use of institutional research departments may well be these administrators' greatest asset.

References

American Association of Community and Junior Colleges. Unpublished Survey Data, 1985.
Anderson, R. A. "Can Community Colleges Offer Opportunity and Excellence?" *Community, Technical, and Junior College Journal,* 1985, 56 (2), 41.
Boyer, E. L. Introduction to F. Newman, *Higher Education and the American Resurgence.* Princeton, N.J.: Princeton University Press, 1985.
Bray, D. "Remediation, Retention, Rigor and Reform—the New 3 R's Plus One." Paper presented at the Northern Adult Education Association, Seattle, Wash., April 17, 1984. 17 pp. (ED 243 534)

Cohen, E. L. *Assessment, Advising and Early Warning: Strategies for Improving Retention.* Santa Barbara, Calif.: Santa Barbara City College, 1984. 22 pp. (ED 243 550)

Coker, R., Donovan, E., Gaskill, M., Watkins, J. F., and Webb, D. *Institutional Retention Study: Gainesville Junior College.* Gainesville, Ga.: Gainesville Junior College, 1985. 40 pp. (ED 257 509)

Duke, D. L. "Decision Making in an Era of Fiscal Instability." *Phi Delta Kappa Fastback,* 1984, *212,* 12.

Eurich, N. P. *Corporate Classrooms: The Learning Business.* Carnegie Foundation for the Advancement of Teaching Special Report. Princeton, N.J.: Princeton University Press, 1985.

Fisher, J. L. *Power of the Presidency.* New York: Macmillan, 1984.

Harrower, G., Jr., Herrling, J. R., Houpt, A., and Maugle, K. B. *Retention: An Inductive Study of Representative Student Groups at Middlesex County College.* Edison, N.J.: Middlesex County College, 1980. 145 pp. (ED 198 851)

Hawley, W. D. "False Premises, False Promises: The Mythical Character of Public Discourse About Education." *Phi Delta Kappan,* 1985, *67* (3), 183-187.

Jones, S. W. *Evaluating the Impact of Freshman Orientation on Student Persistence and Academic Performance.* Fort Lauderdale, Fla.: Nova University, 1984. 40 pp. (ED 241 089)

Keller, A. *Academic Strategy.* Baltimore, Md.: The John Hopkins University Press, 1983.

Keller, L. J., and others. "A Pledge to Educational Access, Excellence, Transferability, and Accountability." A grant proposal to the Colorado Commission on Higher Education, November 1985.

Levitz, R. "Evaluation of Student Retention Programs." Workshop held at the University of Northern Colorado, Greeley, June 1984.

Losak, J., and Morris, C. *Impact of the Standards of Academic Progress on Student Achievement and Persistence at Miami-Dade Community College.* Miami, Fla.: Office of Institutional Research, Miami-Dade Community College, 1983. 21 pp. (ED 239 698)

Myran, G. A. "Strategic Management in the Community College." In G. A. Myran (ed.), *Strategic Management in the Community College.* New Directions for Community Colleges, no. 44. San Francisco: Jossey-Bass, 1983.

National Commission on Excellence in Education. *A Nation at Risk: The Imperative for Education Reform.* Washington, D.C.: U.S. Department of Education, 1983.

National Institute of Education. *The Progress of an Agenda: A First Report from the Study Group on the Conditions of Excellence in American Higher Education.* Washington, D.C.: National Institute of Education, 1984. (ED 244 577)

Newman, F. *Higher Education and the American Resurgence.* Princeton, N.J.: Princeton University Press, 1985.

Reed, J. G. "Dropping a College Course: Factors Influencing Students' Withdrawal Decisions." *Journal of Education Psychology,* 1981, *73* (3), 382-384.

Rounds, J. C. *Attrition and Retention of Community College Students: Problems and Promising Practices.* Marysville, Calif.: Yuba College, 1984. 30 pp. (ED 242 377)

Rumelt, R. P. "Evaluation of Strategy: Theory and Models." In D. E. Schendle and C. W. Hofer (eds.), *Strategic Management.* Boston: Little, Brown, 1979.

P. Anthony Zeiss is president of Pueblo Community College, Pueblo, Colorado.

An emphasis on assessment and accountability is virtually unavoidable if educational leaders are to address the challenge of improved quality and effectiveness.

Assessment of Institutional Effectiveness

Kay McCullough Moore

The recent major debate over the status of American higher education has focused repeatedly and from varying perspectives on the concepts of excellence, quality, and academic standards, often placing those concepts in juxtaposition to the ideals of access and equity. Also pervading the debate has been the mounting call for increased accountability in higher education—for greater strength and precision in the assessment of institutional effectiveness and efficiency in producing the desired outcomes of the educational process.

Emphasis on Effectiveness

The voices have been diverse, the rebuttals often vociferous, and the responses far-ranging. A major stimulus for the discussion has been the plethora of reports from distinguished commissions at the national, regional, and state levels, reports that describe "a nation at risk" (National Commission on Excellence in Education, 1983), call for renewed integrity in the college curriculum (Association of American Colleges, 1985), and propose a variety of recommendations for improvement of quality in undergraduate education (National Institute of Education Study Group, 1984; American Council on Education, 1982; Southern Regional Education

Board, 1985). The reports have generally described a perceived decline in the quality of American higher education (as depicted through standardized test scores, attrition and graduation rates, curricular requirements, and numerous other indicators), which has produced not only a generation of Americans whose educational skills are apparently inferior to those of their elders but also a loss of public confidence in the educational enterprise.

The major reports have been supplemented by a substantial number of publications relating to the importance of liberal education and to issues of curriculum quality in specific discipline areas, particularly science, mathematics, English, and foreign-language studies. Specialized contributions have also come from the various sectors of the higher education system, as exemplified by the 1984 report of the American Association of Community and Junior Colleges' Task Force to Redefine the Associate Degree.

Further impetus for the quest for enhanced quality in higher education has been provided as the regional accrediting agencies for American postsecondary institutions have gradually moved toward a greater emphasis on institutional effectiveness as a criterion for accreditation. Whereas the accrediting agencies traditionally have relied on resource measures as the primary empirical basis for accreditation (equating quality with an institution's resources—bright students, highly qualified faculty, extensive library collections, plentiful dollars), the trend for several years has been toward requirements for greater precision in the statement and assessment of educational outcomes. For example, in 1984 the Commission on Colleges of the Southern Association of Colleges and Schools approved a major revision of the standards used in evaluating the region's postsecondary institutions. What is most significant, the new criteria include a section on "Institutional Effectiveness" which asserts, "The level of institutional quality depends not only on an institution's educational processes and resources but also on the institution's successful use of those processes and resources to achieve established goals. Institutions have an obligation to all constituents to evaluate effectiveness and to use the results in a broad-based, continuous planning and evaluation process" (p. 9). Stipulating that each institution "must define its expected educational results and describe how these results will be ascertained" (p. 9), the criteria also suggest that an effective planning and evaluation process should include broad-based involvement of faculty and administration, the establishment of a clearly defined purpose appropriate to collegiate education, the formulation of educational goals consistent with the institution's purpose, the development of procedures for evaluating the extent to which these educational goals are being achieved, and the use of the results of these evaluations to improve institutional effectiveness. Additionally, institutions are challenged to ascertain periodically the change in the academic achievement of their students and to establish and support institutional research programs for the ongoing assessment of institutional purposes, policies, procedures, and programs.

A major force in the educational reform movement has been the intensive activity of state legislatures across the country. Often amidst great controversy, legislative bodies have appointed select committees, commissioned reports, and acted decisively on reforms in educational finance, access, curriculum, faculty qualifications, admission and graduation requirements, and a variety of related areas. Almost without exception, these measures represent a determination to improve educational quality while causing institutions to become more accountable for the educational outcomes produced.

The writing on the wall is abundantly clear to any community college leader who has been paying attention. The mandate—variously issued by educational professionals, the public, the politicians, and the press—is for increased accountability and increased effectiveness in institutions of higher education. The major challenge now is to discover meaningful and useful ways of distinguishing between effective and ineffective institutions, programs, processes, and even people. That challenge is heightened by the fact that there are multiple domains and dimensions of effectiveness; by the diversity of institutions and the students they serve; and by the extraordinary difficulty of describing the desired outcomes of education and then adequately measuring their achievement.

Because the evaluation of effectiveness is and must remain a task specific to each individual institution, the challenge is quickly brought home to administrators, whose responsibility it is to lead the effort. However, those leaders cannot afford to be deterred from the task by the fact that it is difficult. Rather, it is necessary for them first to develop within the institution a collective understanding of the nature of the task and then to lead the institution through the steps requisite to its achievement. Critical to the success of any effort to evaluate institutional effectiveness is an understanding of the need for and potential contribution of institutional research that is well conceived, properly executed, and appropriately communicated. Offered in the following sections, therefore, are thoughts and guidance intended to assist the administrative leader who seriously assumes the challenge of assessing what is, determining what ought to be, and taking action to bridge the difference.

Asking the Right Questions

All too frequently, discussions of institutional effectiveness become mired in debate over definitions of terms. At the heart of the matter, however, is the relationship of institutional outcomes to institutional goals. As observed by Barnard (1968), "When a specific desired end is attained, we shall say that the action is 'effective' " (p. 19). Similarly, Lawrence (1971) states that "effectiveness refers to the degree to which the program succeeds in doing what was intended" (p. 12).

Many authors emphasize the importance of maintaining a careful distinction between the concepts of effectiveness and efficiency, as characterized, for example, by Ewell: "Efficiency refers to a comparison of resources expended to output produced; it is an assessment of thrift, waste, and prudence. . . . Cost per student credit hour produced is thus a common measure of academic efficiency. Effectiveness, on the other hand, involves comparison of results achieved to goals intended; it is an assessment of the degree to which—regardless of cost—the outcomes . . . measured up to the original intention" (1983, pp. 6-7). Although it is conceptually important to maintain the distinction, both effectiveness and efficiency are concepts that have value and utility to the college administrator. As pointed out by McClenney (1980), the concepts often overlap and in fact may be meaningfully integrated in the notion of productivity. While it is necessary to recognize circumstances in which efficiency may reduce effectiveness (and vice versa), it is also critical to affirm the potential for coexistence of the two concepts in efforts toward institutional improvement.

If, for purposes of the present discussion, it can be agreed that the assessment of effectiveness is based on "comparison of results achieved to goals intended," then it becomes obviously important to acknowledge that not all community colleges—and certainly not all institutions of higher education—are attempting to achieve the same thing. Diversity in institutional mission and goals both produces and reflects the immense diversity in the kinds of students institutions intend to serve. Thus, the assessment of institutional effectiveness must depend fundamentally on each institution's willingness and ability first to ask and then to answer some basic questions: Have we clearly stated what we intend to do? Do we possess a clear understanding of the needs, characteristics, and educational objectives of the students we purport to serve? How well are we doing what we say we are doing? Through the answers to these questions, institutions can document progress toward the achievement of institutional goals and demonstrate accountability to concerned constituencies.

In a college where the issue of effectiveness is to be seriously addressed, there are a number of critical steps to be taken. Fundamentally important are the development of statements of institutional mission and goals, the design and implementation of a systematic process for institutional planning, and the identification of indicators of effectiveness.

Development of Meaningful Statements of Institutional Mission and Goals. While college catalogues and other publications have traditionally included mission statements, it is vitally important that appropriate campus constituencies be involved in the establishment and timely review of statements that accurately describe the enduring purpose, essential functions, and desired goals of the institution. Reaching beyond platitudes, such statements should reflect values and outcomes for which the institution is willing to be held accountable. As Lawrence (1971) points out, a clear statement of mission provides the "yardstick against which to measure effectiveness" (p. 12).

Like mission statements, institutional goals are generally stated in broad, qualitative terms, but they are more specific. As explained by Romney and Bogen (1978), "the goals for an institution represent circumstances sought in pursuit of its mission" (p. 19). Clearly, then, a rigorous effort to define mission and goals provides the essential anchor for institutional planning and evaluation processes.

Design and Implementation of an Institutional Planning Process. After the explication of institutional mission and goals, the next step involves the design and implementation of an ongoing process for institutional planning. Such a process should provide for careful assessment of the college's internal and external environments. In addition to characterizing the institution's current status, the assessment should focus on the identification of forces and factors that will significantly affect efforts toward achievement of institutional goals. The objective here is to describe as clearly as possible the discrepancy between what is and what ought to be—between the institution's present status and performance and the goals it aspires to achieve. Through that assessment, it is possible to identify critical strategic issues that must be addressed if the college is to reduce the discrepancy and to progress toward goal achievement.

Both the assessment process and strategic thinking and decision making are essential to subsequent evaluation of institutional outcomes and effectiveness, because they provide a description of the point of departure, a proposed road map for the journey toward goals achievement, and road signs that alert the college to opportunities to be seized and barriers to be overcome.

With strategic direction established for the institution, the planning process should provide next for the broad involvement of faculty and administrators in the development of shorter-term operational plans, which ensure progress toward strategic objectives. Such plans, developed by each unit of the college for a one- to two-year period, should translate the strategic plan into operational reality and describe the specific steps that must be taken in order to achieve demonstrable progress.

The planning process should continue annually, with the strategic plan first being updated in light of new information, unanticipated developments, and progress achieved and then serving as the basis for generation of operational plans. Operational planning can be the mainstream activity for the assessment of institutional effectiveness in that the effort encompasses the reporting of achievements and results from the immediately preceding year's efforts; the incorporation of findings from ongoing assessments of programs, services, and student learning; and the application of those findings to concrete plans for institutional improvement. According to professional and practical experience, the effectiveness of an institutional planning process will be highly dependent on the extent to which (1) there is opportunity for broad involvement in the development of plans by the faculty and by the administrators who will be responsible for their implementation; (2) there is willingness to undertake the difficult task of establishing priorities; and (3) there are explicit linkages between approved plans and subsequent allocation or reallocation of institutional resources.

Identification of Indicators of Effectiveness. Certainly the most significant challenge in the assessment of institutional effectiveness must be the identification of indicators of effectiveness, criteria chosen to represent the accomplishment of institutional goals. Beyond the articulation of mission and the statement of goals, it is necessary to describe measures, or indicators, that can be used systematically to evaluate the accomplishment of mission and goals. As explained by Fincher (1978), such criteria "are the observed results of institutional or program efforts; they are the quantified, recorded, or otherwise evident aspects of performance, products, and effects that will satisfy skeptics and critics that something called education has taken place" (p. 3).

The identification of effectiveness indicators is made difficult by several factors. First, the assessment of goal achievement is facilitated when organizational goals and outcomes are specific, measurable, consensual, and time-bound. By contrast, educational institutions are often characterized by goals and outcomes that are multiple, complex, ambiguous, and even conflicting. Furthermore, it is often argued (sometimes convincingly) that there are certain desirable outcomes of higher education that simply defy measurement and are devalued in the attempt. It is even postulated that the more significant a goal is, the less amenable that goal will be to measurement. A second source of difficulty is the fact that various constituencies (both internal and external) will have diverse perspectives and opinions about what constitutes effective performance. Finally, there may be widely diverse and even contradictory criteria of effectiveness in different domains of organizational endeavor. Indicators of success in students' personal development, for example, may be irrelevant to or even negatively correlated with effectiveness in academic achievement, community service, and so on.

Because effectiveness is multidimensional and educational outcomes are multiple and diverse, it must be obvious that there can be no single criterion for institutional effectiveness. Rather, the challenge is to achieve consensus regarding appropriate clusters of criteria that are specific and observable and that also make sense to faculty members, administrators, students, policy makers, and the general public.

Institutional Research's Concerns and Contributions

Relating Research to Institutional Mission and Goals. Reflecting on his experience as a "card-carrying institutional researcher," Fenske

(1978) admits to being struck by the frenetic data-gathering activity undertaken in reaction to seemingly endless demands for research from all manner of constituencies. He reports, "Seldom was the question asked: What do the data signify in regard to progress or lack of it toward the mission or goals of the institution . . . ? One barely had time to pause and ask what the data meant: Better or worse, slower or faster growth, less or more effective—than what? According to what criteria?" (p. 80). The questions posed by Fenske, especially if long ignored, must now clearly be brought to the top of the institutional research agenda.

Development of Criteria for Institutional Effectiveness. At hand is the question "How effective is our institution?" The answer obviously depends on the criteria selected for evaluation. As Cameron (1980) notes, "The choice of criteria places boundaries around the concept of effectiveness and gives it a referent" (p. 66). Previous discussion has briefly characterized some of the conceptual and political difficulties impinging on the development of specific criteria or indicators that represent achievement of institutional goals. For the institutional research component, which must serve at least as a technical and conceptual adviser in the process, the concerns are obviously related but more specific. The success of the institution's assessment effort will depend on careful forethought. Cameron (1980) acknowledges that there can be no perfect evaluation, but he further asserts that effectiveness evaluations can be improved if several critical questions are addressed:

1. What domain of activity should be the focus of the evaluation (academic; extracurricular; the area of external/community relationships; the area of morale and satisfaction)?
2. Whose perspective or which constituency's point of view should be considered?
3. What level of analysis should be used: Should assessment data be aggregated at the individual level, at the level of groups or subunits, or for the overall organization?
4. What time frame should be used?
5. What type of data should be used, objective and/or subjective/perceptual?
6. What referent should be employed? Is the evaluation of effectiveness to be based on comparison of organizational performance to performance of other organizations? to a normative standard or theoretical ideal? to the organization's own past performance? to stated organizational goals?

With regard to the actual selection of effectiveness criteria, Romney and Bogen (1978) cite several possible approaches none of which is simple and each of which requires painstaking efforts to relate criteria appropriately to institutional goals. A first possibility is to select measures that are needed or required by state and federal agencies, accrediting associations, licensing boards, and so on. Second, the institution might simply postulate measures that appear to represent the achievement of each institutional goal. Finally, a more sophisticated approach would involve the postulation of some measures, the identification of others in the literature, the description of their linkages to specific goals, and the use of an expert group to verify the linkages as well as determine exactly which measures should be used.

In its research on organizational effectivenes in higher education, the National Center for Higher Education Management Systems has solicited the opinions of college and university administrators, faculty department heads, and trustees in an effort to identify the most important criteria of effectiveness. Among the three groups, the results have indicated strong agreement that certain indicators should be used in any evaluation of institutional effectiveness. Those indicators cluster into nine separate dimensions of effectiveness, as described by Cameron (1980):

> 1. Student educational satisfaction—criteria indicated the degree of satisfaction of students with their educational experiences at the institution.
> 2. Student academic development—criteria indicated the extent of academic attainment, growth, and progress of students at the institution.
> 3. Student career development—criteria indicated the extent of occupational development of students, and the emphasis on career development and the opportunities for career development provided by the institution.
> 4. Student personal development—criteria indicated student development in nonacademic, noncareer-oriented areas, such as social, emotional, or cultural, and the emphasis on personal development and opportunities provided by the institution for personal development.
> 5. Faculty and administrator employment satisfaction—criteria indicated satisfaction of faculty members and administrators with jobs and employment at the institution.
> 6. Professional development and quality of the faculty—criteria indicated the extent of professional attainment and development of the faculty, and the amount of stimulation toward professional development provided by the institution.
> 7. Systems openness and community interaction—criteria indicated the emphasis placed on interaction with, adaptation to, and service in the external environment.
> 8. Ability to acquire resources—criteria indicated the ability of the institution to acquire resources from the external environment.
> 9. Organizational health—criteria indicated benevo-

lence, vitality, and viability in internal processes and practices at the institution [p. 64].

These identified dimensions may provide guidance to the institutional researcher whose responsibility it is to advise and assist administrators and faculty members in criteria development. Further assistance is offered by Fincher (1978), who cautions that selected criteria "should meet the standards of validity, reliability, objectivity, and practicality that predictive or explanatory measures in evaluation research are required to meet" (p. 14) and that "the critieria used in assessing the outcomes and impacts of educational institutions should be educational first and economic, social, or political only in a secondary sense" (p. 5-6).

Practical assistance is also provided in a series of questions proposed by McClenney (1980) for administrative and institutional self-evaluation of "management for productivity." The inventory draws attention, for example, to the importance of mission and goals statements; systematic institutional planning; collection and application of information on student learning and attrition, employee performance and satisfaction, and community needs; and so on. Also very helpful, of course, are descriptions of programs for evaluation of institutional effectiveness that are already well under way in an increasing number of institutions (see, for example, McClain, 1982; Law, 1985.)

Beyond the task of assisting in the identification of effectiveness indicators, the institutional research component should be centrally involved in recommendations pertaining to instrumentation for the evaluation effort. If a valid and reliable instrument does not exist for the measurement of a particular criterion, it may well be desirable to develop one. It could be argued, in fact, that the serious limitations inherent in the use of nationally standardized tests to measure improvement in student academic achievement can best be overcome through the collaborative development of standard departmental examinations especially tailored for and by the individual institution.

Development of an Outcomes Data Base. Administrative leaders and institutional researchers will quickly realize that many of the data necessary to assessment of institutional effectiveness are already available. Most institutions collect a large volume of data for routine operational reports and for special purposes. Often, however, the data may be dispersed throughout the institution, having been collected by different units at different times and for greatly varying purposes. An initial step, therefore, may be simply to create an inventory of available data, indicating how, when, and for what purpose the data were collected. Typically, the institution's existing student data base will include student demographic characteristics, high school GPA and college admission test scores, and college enrollment data (level, major, day/evening, full-/part-time, course load,

Table 1. Commonly Collected Outcomes Data

Source/Location	Type of Data
Academic depts.	Follow-up studies
	Program accreditation reports
Student services	Service evaluations
	Exit interviews
Alumni office	Alumni activity surveys
President's office	Accreditation self-study reports
	Ad hoc studies
Placement office	Placement surveys
	Employer surveys
(Systems offices)	Occupational follow-up studies
	Transfer tracking studies

Source: Adapted from Ewell, 1983.

GPA), as well as the student transcript record. Additional data available from special sources may include aptitude and achievement test scores, educational goals, and survey data reflecting student perceptions of programs and services, student performance in subsequent education, employer satisfaction with education/training provided, and so on. Ewell (1983, p. 32) alerts researchers to "existing outcomes data commonly collected on campus," as shown in Table 1.

A critical task for institutional researchers is the transformation of data into useful information. Drawing on the work of Jones (1982), Ewell explains the distinction: "Data (for example, responses to a questionnaire or the entries in a course-registration file) are the direct results of observation or measurement. They are the raw facts from which information can be constructed. Information, on the other hand, consists of data that have been deleted, combined, and put into a form that conveys to a given recipient some useful knowledge upon which to base action" (p. 27). In the context of the present discussion, the usefulness of information will be determined by its reasonable and demonstrable linkage to particular institutional goals.

As the data inventory is completed, it will surely be observed that there is some unevenness concerning the consistency and accuracy of available data. As the outcomes data base is developed over time, those shortcomings will require attention. Additionally, the researcher will begin to assist faculty and administrators in evaluating the data base in order to identify gaps that need to be filled through new or revised approaches to instrumentation, data collection, and/or data analysis.

Collection, Analysis, and Dissemination of Information. Given clear research objectives and specified criteria for effectiveness, the logistical and technical tasks of data collection and analysis are relatively routine functions of a research component. Beyond the need for well-designed and well-executed studies, however, is a critical key to the success of the process for assessment of institutional effectiveness: clear and meaningful communication of results. Information must be stated in terms that relate criterion measures to institutional mission and goals, make sense to the institution's concerned constituencies, and can be usefully applied in efforts toward institutional improvement.

Conclusion

The purpose of this chapter has been to describe the context for the currently intense interest in the issue of educational effectiveness, to present basic steps to be undertaken in colleges where the assessment of effectiveness is a serious endeavor, and to discuss certain potential contributions of the institutional research component.

It has been asserted that in order to be effective and demonstrate effectiveness, the college must have a clearly stated mission and derivative goals, and that careful attention must then be given to the identification of specific and observable criteria or indicators of effectiveness in goal achievement.

A systematic planning process enables rational consideration of environmental pressures and opportunities, consensus regarding a vision of where the institution wishes to go, and broad involvement of the campus community in determining how it should get there. The planning process becomes a gathering point for various institutional assessment activities, so that information can be integrated, plans for action developed, and priorities established.

To a remarkable extent, educational institutions, although populated by learners, investigators, and evaluators of other organizations, have been heretofore essentially unwilling to assess their effectiveness or to undertake systematic efforts to improve it. In these new times, however, the emphasis on assessment and accountability is virtually unavoidable, and institutional leaders are engaged in a search for positive ways to address the challenge of improved quality and effectiveness. The imperative for that effort is often stated in terms of institutional survival and national well-being. The American Council on Education (1982) report has already stated that higher education's most precious asset is public confidence, and that this asset is in jeopardy. One might be moved to suggest that, in truth, our most precious asset is the entrusted life and mind of the individual student, and that he or she is reason enough.

References

American Council on Education. *To Strengthen Quality in Higher Education.* Washington, D.C.: National Commission on Higher Education Issues, 1982.

Association of American Colleges. *Integrity in the College Curriculum: A Report to the Academic Community.* Washington, D.C.: Project on Redefining the Meaning and Purpose of the Baccalaureate Degree, Association of American Colleges, 1985. 62 pp. (ED 251 059)

Barnard, C. *The Functions of the Executive.* Cambridge, Mass.: Harvard University Press, 1968.

Cameron, K. "Critical Questions in Assessing Organizational Effectiveness." *Organizational Dynamics,* 1980, 9, 66–80.

Ewell, P. *Information on Student Outcomes: How to Get It and How to Use It.* Boulder, Colo.: National Center for Higher Education Management Systems, 1983. 89 pp. (ED 246 827)

Fenske, R. H. "Synthesis and Implications." In R. H. Fenske (ed.), *Using Goals in Research and Planning.* New Directions for Institutional Research, no. 19. San Francisco: Jossey-Bass, 1978.

Fincher, C. "Importance of Criteria for Institutional Goals." In R. H. Fenske (ed.), *Using Goals in Research and Planning.* New Directions for Institutional Research, no. 19. San Francisco: Jossey-Bass, 1978.

Jones, D. P. *Data and Information for Executive Decisions in Higher Education.* Boulder, Colo.: National Center for Higher Education Management Systems, 1982.

Law, W. D., Jr. "Assessing Student Performance: St. Petersburg Junior College." Paper presented at the annual meeting of the Southern Association of Colleges and Schools, New Orleans, December 1985.

Lawrence, B. *Statewide Planning for Postsecondary Education: Issues and Design.* Boulder, Colo.: National Center for Higher Education Management Systems, 1971.

McClain, C. J. *Assessing the Quality of Undergraduate Education.* Kirksville: Northeast Missouri State University, 1982.

McClenney, B. N. *Management for Productivity.* Washington, D. C.: American Association of Community and Junior Colleges, 1980.

National Commission on Excellence in Education. *A Nation at Risk: The Imperative for Education Reform.* Washington, D.C.: U.S. Department of Education, 1983.

National Institute of Education Study Group on the Conditions of Excellence in American Higher Education. *Involvement in Learning: Realizing the Potential of American Higher Education.* Washington, D.C.: U.S. Government Printing Office, 1984.

Romney, L. C., and Bogen, G. K. "Assessing Institutional Goals: Proceed with Caution." In R. H. Fenske (ed.), *Using Goals in Research and Planning.* New Directions for Institutional Research, no. 19. San Francisco: Jossey-Bass, 1978.

Southern Association of Colleges and Schools. *Criteria for Accreditation.* Atlanta, Ga.: Commission on Colleges, 1984.

Southern Regional Education Board. *Access to Quality Undergraduate Education.* Atlanta, Ga.: Commission on Educational Quality, 1985.

Kay McCullough Moore is assistant to the chancellor of the Alamo Community College District in San Antonio, Texas.

The transformation from an industrial society to a technical society based on information is highlighted by illustrations of numerous issues likely to occur in the decade ahead. The most important one is an institution's ability both to assess changes in its external environment and to act on the findings.

Institutional Research and Assessment of the External Environment

Warren H. Groff

The industrial nations of the world are in the turbulent times of a structural shift, from an industrial society based on the physical productivity of material goods to a technical society based on the exchange of ideas, knowledge, and information. The transformation to a new type of society is occurring at a time when this nation is faced with major issues, such as high rates of illiteracy, new waves of immigrants, macrotechnological advances in research and development, plant and industry decay and obsolescence, changes in the workplace, decline in human productivity, escalating human dislocation problems, increasing rates of chemical dependency, high costs of energy and raw materials, and foreign competition in a global economy.

In the past, this nation turned to education as a primary resource in resolving many problems. When society demanded equality of opportunity, education was asked to lead the way through equal access to educational opportunity. When the Soviets launched Sputnik in 1957, education and training systems in the United States were expanded to produce the critical mass of engineers, scientists, and technicians necessary to compete in the space race. When the structural economic transitions began to affect this nation, colleges and universities were called upon to launch programs in economic development and entrepreneurship, technology transfer, and international education and trade.

Much of what was accomplished in educational change can be attributed to the evolution of planning, management, and evaluation technology. In the 1950s, planning had a focus on acquiring more resources and on building facilities for increased numbers of students. In the 1960s, planning had a focus on improving the quality of math and science and producing a sufficient number of scientists and technicians. The 1970s saw the emergence of new demographic trends, social expectations, economic transitions, and dimensions of accountability. As a result, postsecondary education began to adopt the technology of strategic planning and management as a means of institutional advancement (Groff, 1982, 1983).

Strategic Planning and Management

Although the technology of strategic planning and management has been used for years in business and industry and by the federal government and the military, it is still in the early stages of adoption in postsecondary education. This technology for institutional advancement is based on (1) a comprehensive assessment of the institution's external environment (2) a critical analysis or audit of an institution's internal environment, (3) the development of vision and alternative scenarios based on the assessment of the external and internal environments, (4) the selection of strategic options, (5) refinement of the strategic options into tactical alternatives, and (6) the specification and management of strategy to assist the institution's advance toward the preferred scenario. The basic model for strategic planning and management is displayed in Figure 1.

The External Environment

The external environment includes demographic trends, social indicators, economic trends, political change, technological advances, changes in the workplace, information technologies, value shifts, and numerous other variables. The literature indicates at least four techniques for assessing the external environment: needs assessment, market analysis, environmental

Figure 1. Basic Model for Strategic Planning and Management

External
Assessment

Visions ⟶ Strategic ⟶ Tactical ⟶ Strategic
Internal   options   alternatives   management
Audit

scanning, and trend analysis. *Needs assessment* is a generic term used to describe a process for determining the discrepancy between existing and desired levels of attainment with respect to educational goals; it often suggests the need for a new program. *Market analysis* consists of obtaining detailed information about markets or market segments served or unserved by an institution or a system. Market analysis is an organized effort to identify specific wants and needs of market segments and the ways in which institutions meet or could meet them through coherent plans of research, strategy, and communications. *Environmental scanning* consists of sampling and analysis of data about specific areas, such as employment trends, health conditions, literacy, need of the disadvantaged, and so on. *Trend analysis* consists of a systematic review of comparable data, over time, to determine direction. A few examples will illustrate the need for assessing the external environment and set the stage for discussing policy issues.

Demographic Trends. "The greying of America" is the greying of the Baby Boom. The huge group of people born between 1946 and 1964 has been moving toward middle age. These people are 75 million strong—one out of every three Americans, the largest generation in U.S. history. In 1983, the median age of the population reached 30.9 years. On July 1, 1984, the median age of the population was 31.2 years. By the year 2000, the median age of the population is expected to exceed 36 years. The Baby Boomers, when they reached school age, caused classroom and teacher shortages in elementary, secondary, and postsecondary education. Later, they challenged our traditional institutions as young adults, and currently they are transforming workplace values and practices.

The demographic profile varies considerably from state to state and from region to region. Projections show a decline in the number of high school graduates in all but ten states between 1979 and 1995. Eleven states are expected to decline 30 percent or more, and Washington, D.C., expects a decline of 59 percent. In contrast, six states are expected to experience an increase of 10 percent or more, with Utah leading the way (58 percent), followed by Wyoming (49 percent) and Idaho (28 percent).

Institutional funding formulas tend to be student-driven. The role of institutional research is to predict, with some degree of accuracy, the number of persons likely to participate in higher education and the market share for a particular institution. Beyond the direct relationship between number of students and financial support, there are other demographic variables that are useful for making institutional decisions. Information about minority participation, family income, educational attainment, and so on, is of great value in developing policies and programs.

Social Indicators. The values and expectations of people are key determinants of behavior. Understanding what people want to change, and what they hope will remain the same, is vital to policy makers and decision makers.

An individual's welfare in American society depends on that person's ability to work. It is estimated that 90 percent of the present work force will still be working in 1990, and 75 percent of the work force will be working in the year 2000. If predictions prove correct, by 1990, thousands of jobs may be eliminated or drastically changed by advances in science and technology and through tough international competition. In fact, it has been stated that 75 percent of all available jobs in the year 2000 have not even been described yet. Research, however, has documented repeatedly that many employees lack basic education and training for specific jobs that exist in today's world of work.

One important role of institutional research is the assessment of the needs and wants of people in the service area. Analysis of various market segments yields information that can be used by the institution in developing and delivering customized programs to people who might otherwise not seek access to postsecondary education.

Economic Trends. In the early 1800s, this nation experienced a transition from an occupational structure dominated by agricultural and extractive industries, to one dominated by manufacturing and commerce. In the transition from the industrial society to the technical society, there has been a shift of jobs from the manufacturing sector of the economy to the service and information sectors.

The impact of the transition to a technical society is most severe on communities where there was heavy reliance on old manufacturing industries that have felt the sting of international competition or are subject to automation or to unprecedented infusion of contemporary technology into the workplace. The manufacturing industries that are hardest-hit today are primary metals, motor vehicles, household appliances, textiles, footwear, apparel, tire and tubes, electrical distribution, and radio and television receivers. In Ohio, one out of every six manufacturing jobs disappeared between 1977 and 1982, according to data from the economic census program conducted once every five years by the U.S. Census Bureau. In Richland County, Ohio, manufacturing accounted for 51 percent of jobs in 1970 and 41 percent of jobs in 1980; this contrasts with 44 percent and 35 percent for Ohio and 26 percent and 21 percent in the United States for the same period.

In some communities, the economic transition has caused an epidemic of plant shutdowns and left behind a trail of human and community devastation. What has occurred in the past thirty years, however, may be just the beginning. It is conceivable that the period from 1955 to 1985 was the "early postindustrial society" and the period beyond 1985 will be characterized by an even greater explosion of technical advances influencing occupational structure and establishments.

An important role of institutional research is to conduct needs assessments in order to recommend new programs. Institutional research should also monitor economic trends that indicate when existing programs should be modified or eliminated.

Political Change. Institutions of postsecondary education are "of society"—that is, they are created to fill a role that society has deemed necessary to its well-being. Viewed in this light, postsecondary education takes its place alongside elementary and secondary education, human services, government, defense, housing, transportation, and other interests that claim to affect the quality of life and that consume public resources. The education lobby, particularly at the postsecondary level, has not been overwhelmingly successful in elevating education to a top national or state priority. Whatever priority education currently has is attributable, for the most part, to a roster of participants who perceive education and training as a critical variable in solving a number of economic and social problems.

The reports on education have helped to provide the impetus for action at the federal and state levels of government. Reform in education can occur in two essential ways: through leadership by educators, on the basis of sound research, or through political action groups. In both, substantive change must be mediated by a political process in order to obtain the support and resources necessary to bring about meaningful change.

With regard to political process, 76,565 persons serve the fifty states as elected officials. For the most part, they are citizen-legislators who work most of the time at various trades and professions in their home communities and work part-time as lawmakers in state capitals. In addition, there are hundreds of commissions, committees, and task forces at work analyzing societal problems and submitting recommendations about courses of action. It is important to keep tabs on issues, people, and processes. Postsecondary education needs to know where the issue is in its life cycle. Postsecondary education also needs to know how actors in the process size things up. What are the backgrounds, insights, perceptions, moods, and hunches of congressmen, federal officials, legislators, and commission members? What they think will affect what they do. It is impossible for them to be knowledgeable about all issues. Their continuing education cannot be left to chance alone. Their perceptions must be systematically solicited.

In the United States, there is at least one public two-year college in each of 426 of the 435 congressional districts. There are approximately 540 boards that are locally appointed or elected to govern public two-year colleges; in seventeen states, complete legal responsiblity for the governance of public two-year colleges rests with state-level boards, rather than with local governing boards. Governance is even more complex if one considers vocational, technical, and adult occupational education. It is a difficult task to relate the world of education and training to all policy areas, such as health and human services, energy, and transportation. It is equally complex to get diverse governance structures and the education lobby to reach some reasonable consensus in dealing with policy issues, such as the federal role in vocational education, investment in basic and applied research and development, and international education and trade.

Space does not permit a detailed discussion of all aspects of political change. Certainly any comprehensive discussion of this topic would include comment about unions, political action committees, professional lobbyists, and community power structures. Another factor that warrants monitoring is the growth of private educational vendors, including corporate colleges (Eurich, 1985).

Few functions are more important to an institution than the systematic monitoring of political change. It is essential that institutional research provide data about the impacts of federal and state legislation, monitor changes in rules and regulations, generate data to support the applications of financial support, and assess the outcomes of the return on investment in postsecondary education.

Technological Advances. Technology exists for producing almost all durable or nondurable goods and for the delivery of almost every service. Various ways to classify technology have been noted. Edlin (1982) wrote about devices and processes. Watcke (1982-83) developed a list of high technologies. Moody (1982) listed components of the office of the future, or the "paperless office," such as word processing, personal computers, electronic mail, computer-assisted information retrieval, computer output microfilm, facsimile devices, teleconferencing, and reprographics.

In the early 1980s, it was fashionable to use the term *high tech* to describe advanced or contemporary technology. A report of the Joint Economic Committee of the Congress of the United States (1982) indicates:

> High technology industries consist of heterogeneous collections of firms that share several attributes. First, the firms are labor-intensive rather than capital-intensive in their production process, employing a higher percentage of technicians, engineers, and scientists than other manufacturing companies. Second, the industries are science-based in that they thrive on the application of advances in science to the marketplace in the form of new products and production methods. Third, R & D inputs are much more important to the continued successful operation of high technology firms than is the case for other manufacturing industries. Although analysts have reached no general agreement on a definition of high-technology industry, there is a general agreement that the following Standard Industrial Classification (SIC) industries qualify: chemicals and allied products (SIC 28); machinery, except electrical (SIC 35); electrical and electronic machinery, equipment, and supplies (SIC 36); transportation equipment (SIC 37); and measuring, analyz-

ing, and controlling instruments; photographic, medical and optical goods; watches and clocks (SIC 38).

New technology can be applied to every aspect of manufacturing: engineering and design, planning for manufacturing, fabrication and assembly, and marketing and distribution. A detailed listing of components that constitute planning for manufacturing is offered by Kegg (1982).

Most manufacturing activities can be characterized by the quantity of identical products produced as low, medium, or high volume. The word *manufacturing,* for many people, means mass production, or high-volume manufacturing. Actually, low- and medium-volume manufacturing—batch manufacturing—represent at least three-quarters of all industrial production. In spite of this importance, very little automation has been applied to batch processing. Major changes, however, are occurring. To understand these changes, it is helpful to look at contrasting models.

The basic unit for batch manufacturing is a machine with an operator. The role of the worker is to operate the machine by manually adjusting buttons, dials, handwheels, and levers. The machine usually has some sort of electric or hydraulic power. The next advance is electronic intelligence, in the form of computer control, to run the machine accurately, consistently, and repeatedly through a complicated series of operations. Currently the item moves on a journey from machine to machine, to be processed from raw material to part to component to finished product. The journey takes a long time because the item being produced spends 95 percent of the time as inventory—standing in line, waiting, or in transit from machine to machine. New technologies, such as computers and robots, offer opportunities for automating this process.

The transition from today's practice to a fully computer-integrated manufacturing process will take considerable time. State-of-the-art technology is fragmented and consists of individual computer-aided functions that provide greater speed, efficiency, accuracy, and repetition for individual tasks. Data bases are not uniform throughout the series of manufacturing operations. In the factory of the future, computer-aided machines will be sequenced together with automatic handling and transport of materials as they make the journey from raw materials to finished product.

What is important in this discussion is that if an institution chooses to provide customized training services to business and industry, that institution must commit itself to a thorough program of market research. That research must include an understanding of the elements of a particular type of industry—products and services, hard and soft technology, materials and processes, human resources and training needs, management-labor climate, and other variables. Then the institution must commit itself to a sustained effort of organizational development, including development of human resources.

Education and training will always lag behind affluent corporations in the adoption of contemporary technology. The role of institutional research is to monitor advances in science and technology in order to help the college become aware of contemporary technology and then adopt and utilize it.

Changes in the Workplace. In 1940, 20 percent of the jobs in the United States were skilled and required some advanced training; 80 percent were unskilled. In 1984, 80 percent of the jobs were skilled and only 20 percent were unskilled.

The society we now live in requires a work force skilled in new ways. The technical society based on information will require some people who are skilled and flexible and constantly innovating, integrating, and collaborating. How many of us heard of the personal computer and the term *software* before this decade began? How many of us participated in projects that attempted to list data elements required for comprehensive management information systems and then developed educational specifications for mainframes and terminals to mainframes, word processors, and personal computers that would provide accurate, comprehensive, and timely information to persons throughout the workplace?

Several points are important to emphasize. First, not all jobs in the future will be "high tech." It is estimated that only 3 to 5 percent of the jobs will be high tech. Of the ten categories of jobs the Department of Labor predicts will grow in the next decade, not a single one is high tech (Levin and Rumberger, 1985). Second, 80 percent of the new jobs are created by establishments less than four years old and with twenty or fewer employees. The *Fortune* 500 industries have not created a net new job in the last decade. Third, one in five persons is functionally illiterate, and two additional persons in five are marginally illiterate. These statistics, however, relate only to traditional definitions of illiteracy, including reading comprehension and basic arithmetic, and do not extend to such areas as writing, speaking, and listening, not to mention occupational research, information processing, and economic, scientific, and technological illiteracy.

Changes in types of work require a capability to go beyond the collection of data on the number of establishments and jobs in a service area. There must be a way to look at levels of technology development and to interpret changes in competencies and skills in various occupations. One way to deal with levels of technology development would be simply to classify technology, using such categories as low, medium, and high, and then specify the technology that fits each level. An institution can then begin to interpret the skill levels required to maintain existing levels of technological development, as well as the competencies required to raise a group of establishments in a service area to a higher level.

Another task relates to interpreting the impact of change on occupations. Helms (1982) classifies occupations as obsolete, obsolescent, current, emerging, and emergent. Advances of information and related technologies are having a profound impact on occupational structures in the United States. If predictions prove correct, by 1990 thousands of jobs may be eliminated or drastically changed by advances in technology. In addition, it has been estimated that 75 percent of all available jobs in the year 2000 have not even been described yet. Finegold (1984) listed 160 job titles that might appear in the *Dictionary of Occupational Titles* of the future. It is important to identify changes in the workplace and then to develop programs to upgrade the existing work force and to retrain displaced workers for emerging or emergent occupations.

Contemporary technology means new competencies and skills. Institutional research can assist departments to anticipate changes in science and technology and then to interpret their impact on curricula.

Information Technologies. Advances in information technologies are so important that they deserve a separate category. Their importance can be seen in the development of television over the past several decades. In the late 1940s and early 1950s, we had broadcast television. Viewers watched programs at the time they were broadcast, live from place of origin. The black-and-white picture was projected onto a small screen without sharp definition. In 1964, we first saw an international Olympics live. Today, we routinely watch the instantaneous dramas of war on the other side of the globe, hijacked airliners, or the starving children anywhere in the world.

The importance of the uses of information technology should not be underestimated. The quality of courseware packages that have been developed over the past few years has been improving steadily. Programmed Logic for Automatic-Teaching Operations (PLATO), which began in 1960 at the University of Illinois, now has seventy full systems outside Control Data's own proprietary training institutions, fifty of them in industry. Some form of PLATO is being used at more than two hundred colleges and universities. Computer-based training systems have increased at a phenomenal rate; forty-seven major corporations participated in the Computer-Based Training Conference and Exposition last year. In addition, information-based systems are on the increase. Examples include NewsNet, BidNet, SchoolNet, BitNet, MailNet, PenNet, Open/Net, OHIONET, EASYLINK, and INFO-LINE. Graduates of postsecondary education will be expected to know how to use information-based systems and how to use technology-based systems to continue their education and training and become lifespan learners, remediating their own deficiencies through technology-based systems. Graduates will be expected to be able to access data and information and become knowledge engineers and, in some instances, human resource development engineers for other employees they supervise.

The primary function of a college is to enhance learning through effective and efficient instruction. In the future, communication and information technologies will be used extensively to enhance learning. Institutional research can play a vital role in the improvement of learning through evaluation.

Value Shifts. The term *value* has multiple definitions. The way it is used in this context relates to the usefulness or importance of something to an individual, such as the value of a good college education or the traditional values of American life. Numerous persons have attempted to classify values, develop scales to measure values, study the change in values as people progress through various stages of development, and study different value systems within organizations. The intent here is not to review a great deal of research on values. Rather, a few facts will be presented, along with several comments on the need to include something about values in assessing the external environment.

The American Association of State Colleges and Universities (1978) developed *A Futures-Creating Paradigm* as a way of planning futures and bringing planning assumptions into focus. The project uses a cross-influence matrix of twelve societal trends and twelve values to determine goals in ten areas. Elfrey (1982, p. 11) developed a list of values and themes in a study that attempted to analyze things that really matter at work. Such projects are useful in developing the list of values an institution will assess systematically.

The need to assess values in the external environment is extremely important. In 1984, Americans' personal disposable income rose 6.9 percent, to $3 trillion. The per capita personal disposable income reached its highest level, but the priority of education for the use of that discretionary income dropped. Consider these facts:

- The percentage of women postponing childbirth or deciding not to have children is increasing.
- The number of female-headed households has more than doubled since 1960, from 4.5 million to almost 10 million in 1982.
- In 1980, women living in poverty constituted 16.5 percent of total female population and nearly two-thirds of all students living in poverty.
- Nearly 40 percent of female-headed households live in poverty; half of all the poor live in these households.
- In 1983, nearly 80 percent of working women were in clerical sales, factory, or service jobs, earning 61¢ to every man's dollar.
- A survey showed that 43 percent of Americans said they would have trouble paying an unexpected bill of $1,000.
- The median level of savings and investment fell to $4,600 from $5,700 in 1983.
- In the 1982 congressional elections, fewer than 30 percent of the potential college student voters went to the polls.

These facts are the elongated shadow of values and are a good prediction of the way people will act. Values influence both choices and allocation of resources. Institutional research can play a valuable role in providing educational decision makers with information about the values held by people in their service areas.

Summary and Conclusion

The focal concepts in this chapter are several. First, the structural economic shift, from an industrial society to a technical society, is providing impetus for the adoption of a new technology for managing our institutions, a technology that includes a comprehensive assessment of the external environment in order to develop a vision of the future and preferred scenarios. Second, each institution and system must adopt the technology of strategic planning, management, and evaluation to fit its unique needs, including the specification of categories of variables to be collected and analyzed. Third, postsecondary education is only in the early stages of the adoption of this management technology; to reach full maturity, we must elevate our sights and expectations from a concentration on counting historical, quantifiable internal and external variables to creating preferred futures with an expanded roster of participants through new alliances and partnerships.

Numerous policy issues arise. First, postsecondary education must exercise leadership in sustaining the educational reform movement. The emerging technology of strategic planning, management, and evaluation is presented as a potential tool for dealing with that issue. Second, the educational reform movement must deal simultaneously with equality and excellence. Equality must include variations in age, geography, and handicap. Rewarding excellence and achievement must be matters of public policy. Third, accountability must be based on expectations set forth in clear statements of mission and essential purposes and then projected into the multiyear plans of action, with long-term goals, short-range objectives, and resource requirements. Then, evaluation must be based on performance appraisal that includes outcomes (both outputs of establishments and impacts on service areas) and should be verified through the accreditation process. Fourth, and perhaps most important, is the issue of creating visions of the future and managing change. Purposeful human activity and meaningful resource allocation can occur only when there is vision and hope. American managers in business and education are trained primarily in directing dynamic growth, measured in quantifiable variables—full-time equivalent (FTE) students, head counts, size of mainframe, number of terminals per FTE, and so on. Many schools and colleges have been trimming the fat, and some have gone into bankruptcy. Managing the downside is a much tougher task than directing dynamic growth. In the long run, this form of natural selection can produce a stronger American education and training industry. It will require the critical mass of intellectual capital to create visions and will have profound policy implications for colleges of education that produce professional educators and leaders, particularly higher education administrators.

In conclusion, numerous issues will be important in the decade ahead. No issue will be more important, however, than the relationship between postsecondary education and the society of which it is a part. That relationship can be determined only if postsecondary education makes a commitment to the assessment of its external environment. Gollattscheck and others (1976) state the mission of community renewal as follows:

> We believe the time has come for a ... major development in American postsecondary education: the creation of the community renewal college. The deterioration of our communities, the increasing inability of individuals to cope with rapid change, the obsolescence of individuals and social organizations, and the increasing number of citizens with educational needs who are beyond the purview of existing colleges demand a new kind of postsecondary institution. This new college must be committed to the improvement of all aspects of community life [p. x-xi].

References

American Association of State Colleges and Universities. *A Futures-Creating Paradigm: A Guide to Long Range Planning from the Future for the Future.* Washington, D.C.: American Association of State Colleges and Universities, 1978.

Edlin, W. "High Technology's Impact on Education." *The Associate,* 1982, *1* (3), 8-9.

Elfrey, P. *The Hidden Agenda: Recognizing What Really Matters at Work.* New York: Wiley, 1982.

Eurich, N. P. *Corporate Classrooms: The Learning Business.* Princeton, N.J.: The Carnegie Foundation for the Advancement of Teaching, 1985.

Finegold, S. N. "Emerging Careers: Occupations for Post-Industrial Society." *The Futurist,* 1984, *18* (1), 9-16.

Gollatscheck, J. F., Harlacher, E. L., Roberts, E., and Wygal, B. R. *College Leadership for Community Renewal.* San Francisco: Jossey-Bass, 1976.

Groff, W. H. "Entrepreneurship Through Strategic Planning, Management, and Evaluation." *Trustee Quarterly,* 1982, *6* (2), 12-17.

Groff, W. H. "Strategic Planning." In G. A. Myran (ed.), *Strategic Management in the Community College.* New Directions for Community Colleges, no. 44. San Francisco: Jossey-Bass, 1983.

Helms, W. C. (president, Occupational Forecasting, Inc.). Comments made at Annual Conference of American Vocational Association, St. Louis, Mo., 1982.

Joint Economic Committee of the Congress of the United States. *Location of High-Technology Firms and Regional Economic Development.* Washington, D.C.: U.S. Government Printing Office, 1982.

Kegg, R. (director of Machine Tool Development, Cincinnati Milacron). Presentation made at the University of Cincinnati, October 20, 1982.

Levin, H. M., and Rumberger, R. W. "Technology's Future Impact on the Nation's Workplace." *School Shop*, 1985, *44* (9), 55-60.

Moody, H. G. "The Face of the Future: The Office." *VocEd*, 1982, *57* (1), 36, 83.

Watcke, R. R. "Partnership Vital to High Tech." *Community and Junior College Journal*, 1982-83, *53* (4), 28-31.

Warren H. Groff is director of research and development at North Central Technical College, Mansfield, Ohio.

Two administrators who use the products of institutional research offer their views on the integral relationships among the chief executive, the institutional research department, and the public relations department.

Campus Leadership: Managing and Marketing Through an Effective Institutional Research Program

J. Terence Kelly, Ann M. Otto

Effective campus leadership in the current era of American higher education is now more than ever predicated on new knowledge and skills in marketing, in conjunction with an understanding of and appreciation for the proper use of an efficient institutional research program. This is not to imply that traditional skills necessary for sound campus management are no longer needed, but rather to suggest that these long-recognized traits must now be augmented by research data that are traditional as well as new and imaginative in scope. With this orientation, it is imperative that there be an amalgamation of campus leadership and research findings if community college campuses are to continue to retain their positions as innovators in higher education.

Too often, institutional research, public relations, and the functions of presidents' offices have tolerated each other, at one extreme, and coexisted on an uneven mutual-need basis dictated by time and circumstance, at the other extreme. The central theme of this chapter is that the health and vitality of an institution is to a large extent directly proportional to the integration of the comfort and confidence levels of those selling the campus, those conducting research about the campus, and those leading the campus.

Demographics

All good managers have traditionally been interested in and conversant with the demographics of their student populations. Where do the students come from, and why do they enroll? Knowledge about the types of high schools from which the students graduate, how they find out about the institution, and what are successful recruiting techniques are critical data that all good campus managers need to have readily available.

Curriculum trends, shifting enrollment patterns, and the composition and nature of the student body are some of the more obvious institutional research data that are necessary for decision making. There is simply no substitute for basic demographic data that can be collected and presented in an unlimited variety of configurations.

One of the overwhelming factors in the University of Texas national study that led to Miami–Dade Community College's selection as "America's Number One Community College" was the extraordinary number of data the college had collected about its students (Roueche and Baker, 1985). There was simply more known about what happened to its students, from start to finish, than at any similar institution. College researchers plotted the progress of students at every level. Test scores were catalogued and cross-referenced with students who were mandated into developmental work. Data were generated as to how well students persisted in the institution, how well they did in individual classes, and how well they did beyond the institution, either in the university setting or in the workplace. Employers were queried concerning graduate performance, and suggestions were made concerning program modification. Responsiveness to the demands of an ever-changing technological society has enabled Miami–Dade to retain a very dynamic curriculum. Thus, simply knowing what happens to the students and knowing the community reaction to those students and their skills forms an important data base for the campus manager intent on moving an educational institution forward.

Providing Useful Configurations of Data from Test Results

Data from results of student testing are probably some of the most difficult information to manage. Obviously, the data have to be collected in the most professional manner, but how to use the data properly can become an issue. Communicating and interpreting test information to individuals who are not generally familiar with percentiles, medians, modes, rankings, raw scores, and other kinds of statistical jargon requires special skills to bring meaning to any public discussion of test data. While the research office personnel may well present the data in the ways in which they are professionally most comfortable, it is the responsibility of the educational leader, when addressing a lay audience, to make certain that they understand both the presentation and the interpretation of the data.

An illustration of this principle occurred when the test data on entry-level students at Miami-Dade Community College indicated that about 60 percent were deficient in one or more basic skills (Davis, 1985). It would have been tempting for the college president simply to release the scores and accuse the high schools of not doing their jobs. Instead, in conjunction with the local superintendent of schools, he chose to call a joint meeting of the school board and the college board of trustees to present the data in a nonthreatening, nonaccusatory fashion. They discussed what the data meant and pledged that both systems would work out a solution to the problem ("Education Goes Cooperative," 1982). This was viewed in a very positive manner by both systems, which enabled them to move forward together. Had the data been released strictly through a research report, and not interpreted or adjusted in such a way as to temper their potentially severe consequences, all factions could have suffered.

In the early 1980s, Miami-Dade Community College implemented a comprehensive program of education reforms (Lukenbill and McCabe, 1978). The question that has often been asked is how such a massive undertaking was accomplished. The fundamental answer can be found by understanding the prominent role of college leadership throughout the entire process, as well as the close relationship between public relations and institutional research. Two specific projects illustrate this point.

Before a mandatory entry-level assessment program was established at Miami-Dade Community College, for several semesters there was pilot testing of various instruments to indicate the types of remedial work that would be required. Using the College Guidance Placement battery of the College Board, national and local norms of the test, and local "gaming" techniques, the institutional research office was able to predict, with a high degree of accuracy, the number of students who would have one or more deficiencies in basic skills. Without this type of research documentation, chaos would have prevailed, and the institution would not have had sufficient time to organize a major shift from college-level work to a pre-college-level program. This type of information has to be merged with data about the teaching faculty and their skills and aspirations for teaching in the developmental program. Without this type of research, planning, and decision making, there could be false expectations for the students and the institution; institutions might test students, and discover their deficiencies, yet be unable to produce programs to remediate their weaknesses. If an institution cannot match an educational program with test results, it may do better not to test in the first place.

Another example of how a potentially explosive situation was turned around occurred in the same academic-reforms arena, involving public relations, institutional research, and the president's office. An important component of the educational reform program at Miami-Dade Community College was the adoption of a new standard of academic progress. Institutional research personnel proceeded to "game out" the data—that is, to ask what the impact would be if a program of this nature were to be implemented. With regard to this effort, the impact projected was fairly severe for large numbers of students, particularly for all minority students and even more so for native American and black students. The public relations office became involved. Those with leadership responsibilities tried to take these data and interpret them positively, to indicate that if this program were put in place, it would give the institution a much better opportunity to monitor the progress of students and to enhance long-term success. To show students that there was deepening concern about their progress, early-warning systems were installed and publicized to the community, in light of the positive effect this could have on students' progress through the institution. An effort was being made to stop the "revolving door" accusation that has been leveled at community colleges, particularly those that enroll large numbers of minority students. Before the program was inaugurated, the public relations office managed to inform the community and thereby garner strong public support. There were favorable editorials from the leading black newspaper in Miami ("Basics on the College Level," 1978) and several other papers, magazines, television, and radio stations (Whited, 1982; "Minimum Standards at Miami-Dade," 1978). A great deal of this can be attributed to, and is an illustration of, a sound working relationship among the various offices of public relations, research, and campus leadership.

With respect to exit-level testing, a far-ranging educational program, with a resounding potential for either positive or negative impact, has been the implementation of the College-Level Academic Skills Test (CLAST) in Florida. It is probably fair to point out that the pluses and minuses of the program relate to one's own value system. The CLAST is a state-imposed test that determines whether students will receive the associate degree and be allowed to progress to the junior level within the state university system. It is applied across the board to community college and university students.

While the raw test scores emerge from the state, there is considerable institutional research data that can be effectively used to improve individual educational programs. The CLAST data, if used in conjunction with entry-level test information, can provide information on how effectively the open-door college operates. At Miami-Dade Community College, for example, the latest CLAST data show, in conjunction with Miami-Dade base data, that approximately 34 percent of those who started with one or more basic-skills deficiencies were able to pass all portions of the CLAST and thus receive the associate degree and advance to the university level (Belcher, 1984). Results such as these make a definite statement about the quality of a developmental program and an open-door process.

In addition, the exit-level test scores can describe something about the pattern of studies. As both Broward and Miami-Dade Community Colleges' research has clearly demonstrated, if there occurred in the students' transcripts certain patterns of prescribed classes, students had an extraordinarily high chance of passing the CLAST test. Conversely, if they did not pass the sequence of courses that the college suggested, their chances of passing the CLAST were much more limited. Looking behind the institutional data, one can also find instructors with recognizable success rates of students passing the various English and math portions of the CLAST. Likewise, there is also a pattern emerging that identifies instructors who have inordinate numbers of students who do not achieve at acceptable levels on the CLAST.

Data such as these are essential if faculty upgrading and program enhancement are to be pursued by concerned campus administrators. Generation of these data by the office of institutional research and effective communication of the findings by the offices of the college president and public relations strengthen the argument for extensive cooperation among the three areas.

Student Satisfaction

One of the fundamental lessons to be learned from recent major research on corporations (for example, Peters and Waterman, 1982) is that companies that knew as much as possible about how their customers felt about their services were the companies that tended to be most successful. Companies that continually attuned themselves to customer satisfaction were enterprises that were able to respond better to needs. Probably the weakest area in most educational institutions is knowledge about students' satisfaction with admissions and registration, class experiences, extra-curricular associations, and other experiences, up to graduation. If there is an area that needs work, institutional research officers, along with leadership and marketing individuals, ought to be continually concerned with how well students think their educational experiences are going. Periodic surveys should ask first-term students (and beyond) about the strengths and weaknesses of the institution, and the campus leadership should be able to make adjustments in the educational program, when they are clearly indicated. What can we really say about how students feel about the hospitality or friendship levels of a campus? How much do we know about how well staff, particularly classified staff, feel they are rendering services? Do we make a conscientious effort to find out what they think is the central important issue of the enterprise of teaching and learning? Do we survey faculty often enough about their satisfaction in working at the institution? Do we really know a great deal about what takes place in educational institutions on an ongoing, day-to-day basis?

Broward Community College has recently initiated efforts to improve marketing of the institution's services. In developing a long-range plan for marketing the institution and recruiting students, it was essential to know why students had enrolled and how satisfied they were with the educational program and services. First-time-in-college students, and those who were re-enrolling after an absence of twelve or more months, were mailed the survey. To encourage responses, students who responded by a certain date had their names placed in contention for acquiring a free class.

The survey was designed so that the responses could be tabulated on the campus that students attended. Thus, for a four-campus operation serving 30,000 students, the institution could assess such functions as library services, student development, learning laboratories, and a variety of other support services on the basis of student satisfaction by campus. Survey questions also supplied answers to whether marketing efforts provided by radio, television, and newspaper advertisements had reached appropriate audiences (Mehallis, 1986).

Community

Does the institution really know how the community views it? Is it well thought of? Is it well understood in terms of its goals, mission, and services? Often colleges neglect the very communities they are supposed to serve. How can we collect such information and share it with the appropriate people? If individuals who have responsibility for marketing an institution are not really familiar with the perceptions and views of the community it serves, how can the college be expected to develop an effective and meaningful marketing program? Where are the concerns, misunderstandings, or negative feelings that are consistent throughout the community? How can that information be digested so that decision makers can attune themselves to problems? In many communities, there are survey functions available through local news media, such as newspapers. Generally, industries involved in informing the public must also survey the public on perceived community needs and expectations. Community colleges have recently begun taking advantage of these media surveys by adding questions to survey instruments, seeking to determine levels of community satisfaction with and recognition of community college programs. In most cases, raw data from community-based surveys can be assimilated by the institutional research area and integrated into an institution's marketing approach.

Sharing data with the community about student preferences is an effective means of building solid community relations. At Miami-Dade, the new academic-standards program, which could have been an explosive issue within the black community, was further defused by the reporting of results that showed how the most substantial gains in the key categories after a three-year period were obtained by black students. This was important information for community leaders, who then had a better understanding of what was taking place in the institution (McCabe, 1983).

Institutional Research Directions

When marketers, institutional researchers, and educational decision makers meet on a regular basis, the institution benefits. Too often, educational researchers have their own areas of interest, unrelated to major problems or concerns that the institution's leadership faces. Likewise, marketers are often unequipped with information about what is working and not working in the institution. Therefore, attending to the kinds of resources that are put into institutional research is a critical administration decision. An interesting experiment occurred at Miami-Dade Community College when, in the last accreditation process, the traditional self-study was abandoned for an opportunity to evaluate the educational reform program that was implemented in the early part of the 1980s. Institutional research supported faculty-driven questions evaluating the success of the new education reform program. With sound research techniques, questionnaires were developed to answer myriad concerns raised by the faculty. Faculty in each discipline, students, clerical staff, administrators, legislators, and business and community leaders were all surveyed, from a variety of perspectives, on how well the educational reforms were being received. This approach, augmented by other standard research applications, became the heart of the self-evaluation process that emerged for accreditation.

Conclusion

When one analyzes the current problems facing American society, one can easily see how community colleges must be relied upon for solutions. Certainly the plight of minorities would have to be at the top of the list. Educators must find ways to increase the level of education of minorities and contribute toward building a long-range base for continued economic development. How institutions are able to respond to this need will depend a great deal on how much they know about their minority neighborhoods and their minority constituents. What are the specific problems regarding housing, transportation, and related issues? The more the institution knows about these issues, the better it will be able to respond. Likewise, the marketing of the local campus in minority neighborhoods is a key to acceptance and endorsement. What is attractive to minorities, and how best to recruit these populations, are questions for institutions to ask and answer, using the resources of an office of institutional research. Again, a three-way partnership among decision makers, public relations personnel, and institutional researchers is needed to address this particular problem.

Community colleges clearly will need to know more about how all students perceive their educational experiences, whether there is a genuine level of caring, and whether students view their learning as essential or trivial. All these questions can be answered by an effective institutional research program. The campus administration is then charged with turning data into programs and services that are responsive to recognized and documented needs.

Institutions that will be effective in the coming era will have to know much more about what takes place in the classroom. More definitive data must be obtained on the effectiveness of various instructional methods. Establishing a climate for excellence is the responsibility of the chief executive officer. This cannot be accomplished, however, without collaboration from the faculty and support staff. The Roueche and Baker (1986) community college model for understanding and evaluating organizational effectiveness is an integration of well-executed market research and superior leadership.

With increased demand for improvement in all segments of education, it is incumbent upon community college leaders to organize their institutions so as to maximize research and marketing dollars and guarantee "truth in advertising" for the programs and services that comprise their institutional missions. This is a fascinating time, a time that suggests that institutional research personnel who deal with objective, raw data must cooperate with those who have responsibility for marketing and managing the institution, to ensure the highest level of integrity and overall excellence throughout the organization.

References

"Basics on the College Level." *The Miami Times,* June 22, 1978.

Belcher, M. *A Cohort Analysis of the Relationship Between Entering Basic Skills and CLAST Performance for Fall 1981 First-Time-in-College Students.* Miami, Fla.: Office of Institutional Research, Miami-Dade Community College, 1984. 33 pp. (ED 267 870)

Davis, D. *MAPS Entry-Level Basic Skills Test Outcome for First-Time-in College Students at Miami-Dade Community College, Fall Term, 1985.* Miami, Fla.: Office of Institutional Research, Miami-Dade Community College, 1985.

"Education Goes Cooperative: M-DCC, Dade Plan Learning Marriage." *The Miami News,* December 16, 1982, section A, p. 5.

Lukenbill, J., and McCabe, R. *General Education in a Changing Society.* Dubuque, Iowa: Kendall/Hunt, 1978.

McCabe, R. "A Status Report on the Comprehensive Educational Reform of Miami-Dade Community College." Document reported to community leaders, Miami, March 1983.

Mehallis, M. *Student Marketing Information Survey.* Ft. Lauderdale, Fla.: Broward Community College, 1986.

"Minimum Standards at Miami-Dade." Editorial WPLG-TV, Channel 10, June 27, 1978.

Peters, T., and Waterman, R. *In Search of Excellence: Lessons from America's Best-Run Companies.* New York: Harper & Row, 1982.

Roueche J., and Baker, G. "The Success Connection Toward Equality with Excellence." *Community and Junior College Journal,* 1985, *55,* 18-22.

Roueche, J., and Baker, G. "The Success Connection Examines the Fruits of Excellence." *Community and Junior College Journal,* 1986, *56,* 47-56.

Whited, C. "Get-Tough Stand Putting M-DCC on Honor Roll." *The Miami Herald,* February 2, 1982, section B, p. 1.

J. Terence Kelly is vice-president for the North Campus at Miami-Dade Community College in Miami, Florida.

Ann M. Otto is vice-president for development at Broward Community College, Broward, Florida.

In the next decade, the greatest need of institutions with research capabilities may be not only to cope with change, but also to influence change through the systematic generation and presentation of data.

Meeting the Challenge of Change: An Opportunity for Research in the Community College

Edith H. Carter

The focus of this chapter will be directed toward citing key areas for research within the institution, as determined from a review of recent literature. It is the purpose of this chapter to challenge researchers and administrators about the need for applied research within the institution in order to respond to the ever-increasing number of external and internal forces challenging higher education, and especially community colleges, today. The author's conceptualization has been heavily influenced by Stevenson and Walleri (1981).

Institutional research in the community college has been constantly changing by responding to the needs of different periods. During the 1960s, as community colleges grew, research was a source of information about the institution for administrators and the public. In the 1970s, research was generally concerned with learning the new technologies, as institutions grew and the requirements for reports from state and federal agencies increased. Stabilizing enrollments in the late 1970s and early 1980s caused research to be directed toward impact studies and business and industry relations. Many researchers also had to be concerned about marketing strategies, budget and finance, and fundraising.

With increased emphasis on accountability, community colleges are facing some of the greatest challenges in their history. The next decade will be a period of response to those challenges. It is the intent of this chapter to challenge those in research-related positions to conduct institutional analysis studies that can be used to respond to some of those issues in higher education. The greatest needs of the next decade may not be recruitment, marketing, or fundraising, but rather responsiveness to the needs of students, faculty, and the community.

A Period of Growth

For the past three decades, higher education has been challenged by the external forces of economic change, limited finances, changes in lifestyles, and population demographics (Eaton, 1984). Throughout much of the period after World War II, higher education in general, and community colleges in particular, were part of a rapid-growth industry that experienced large gains in resources and enrollments. During the period between 1961 and 1980, the number of community colleges almost doubled, from 687 to 1,233, and the number of students increased from 750,000 to 4.8 million. In this growth period, community colleges developed as comprehensive institutions whose mission was tied to the educational needs of the communities they served (Nielsen and Polishook, 1982). There were few who questioned the value of college education. College education opened the door to a future of virtually unlimited job opportunities and high social mobility (Linthicum, 1982).

Community colleges expanded their programs to provide opportunities for anyone desiring higher education. Students were given the freedom to choose courses, faculty experimented with teaching methods, and courses of questionable academic value were suddenly being counted for credit toward graduation. The buzz words were *access* and *opportunity*. Research studies revealed many benefits to society through the growth and expansion of higher education.

During the 1970s, community college enrollments began to stabilize, and changing demographics began to have a profound effect on the missions and goals of community colleges. The declining birthrate and the steady decrease of high school graduates have resulted in a steady state, or declining enrollments. External factors of limited financing, economic change, and shifts in life expectations and life-styles are reshaping community college education. There is a growing concern that society can no longer afford education for the masses. The theme of the open door is being replaced with those of limited access, quality, and excellence. The concept of quantitative growth has been replaced with that of qualitative growth. Nielsen and Polishook (1982) pose three questions relating to quality: Have community colleges overextended the services they can offer? Are community colleges too expensive for their constituents? Are students enrolled and graduated at the expense of academic excellence?

During the fall of 1984, a National Institute of Education study group (Mortimer, 1984) delineated basic education problems, including inadequate preparation and achievement of undergraduates; student attrition; vocationalization of the curriculum; and retrogression of support for the academic structure in such areas as ratios of full-time to part-time faculty, faculty salaries, equipment, and research facilities. This report, unlike others that came out around the same time (for example, Nielsen and Polishook, 1984), provided positive rather than negative measures for improving coherence in the curriculum, student learning, academic standards, and upgrading of facilities.

The report stressed that American education should be broadened to provide "increased opportunities for intellectual, cultural, and personal growth of all our citizens" (Mortimer, 1984, p. 35). Another issue of concern in this report was access. Many Americans are currently undereducated in relation to potential; access should be extended to larger segments of the population, regardless of age. Another concern was reducing the dropout rate of students; only slightly over half of the students who enter higher education eventually graduate. American society must use all the means available to encourage willing students to continue learning. While institutions have conducted rather random follow-up studies of dropouts and nonreturning students, little if anything has been done to respond to the minimal research conducted in this area. The report goes on to state:

> Greater access to higher education will be meaningless, if colleges, community colleges, and universities do not offer high-quality programs to their students. True equity requires that all Americans have access to quality higher education—to programs that demand college-level learning, that provide meaningful contact between faculty and students, and that serve as guides for intelligent action in the world beyond the campus.
>
> To assure excellence, our colleges, community colleges, and universities should maintain high standards of student and institutional performance. The results (or "outcomes") of these institutions must be measured against their clearly and publicly articulated standards of performance.
>
> Since excellence can be attained in diverse educational contexts, diversity in the missions of our colleges, in the specific means by which quality education is achieved, and in the composition of student, faculty, and administrative bodies should be preserved . . . diversity should never serve as a

method for limiting opportunities or lowering expectations [Mortimer, 1984, p. 35].

Amid the prevalence of reports on education that blame teachers and administrators for problems in education, the public must be made aware of the undermining of quality that is attributable to bad times. Educators are painfully aware of the impact of federal and state funding cutbacks, declining enrollments, uncertain budgets, and the effects of retrenchment on academic freedom and tenure, which diminish the objectivity necessary for the academic community (Nielsen and Polishook, 1984).

Access and Quality

Community college students of the 1980s include adults, women, ethnic minorities, senior citizens, the handicapped, foreign students, and high school graduates who are entering college for the first time. Institutions have assumed the implementation of special programs and services for students with specialized backgrounds. One of the problems of program development for these students has been to assess the impact of programs on those students (Hall and Reed, 1981). Until recently, the emphasis has been on meeting the growth demands of these student populations, and not on measuring the effectiveness of new programs and services.

Thompson (1985) suggests that in many institutions of higher education there is a shift in emphasis from open access to quality, which gives the impression that the two concepts are diametrically opposed to each other. The new emphasis on quality has come about because of a general national criticism of public education and limited economic resources. The long-term effect of inquiry may have a substantive impact on open-door admissions if institutions believe they must choose between access and quality.

Society has become accustomed to measuring institutional quality on the basis of specialized curricula, productivity in research, and high admissions selectivity, all of which are uncharacteristic of the community college (Palmer, 1983-84). Open admission provides a second chance to students who, either by circumstance or by choice, did not follow the traditional path to higher education. Quality should be measured not by who is admitted but by what is produced (Thompson, 1985).

Stabilized enrollments and decreased funding have placed a new emphasis on quality and excellence in recent years. How community college observers and practitioners measure quality is a complex issue. Palmer (1983-84), in a review of the literature, identified five determinants as quality indices: student outcomes, value-added impact on students, institutional resources, curriculum emphasis and structure, and management and instructional processes.

While a large number of articles and presentations discuss quality, relatively few present methodologies for measuring quality. In the few that utilize methodologies, there are basically three measurement techniques: value-added measures, decision-making techniques, and outcomes measures. It is evident that additional research is needed to gain empirical knowledge on the question of quality (Palmer, 1983-84).

Open admission is not contrary to the achievement of quality. Having both open admission and quality outcomes is desirable. The path the student follows after admission, and the achievement of quality, will both depend on the entering skills of the student, the college resources available, and the ability and desire of the student to succeed (Thompson, 1985).

A study by Belcher and Losak (1985) of students who would have been initially ineligible to enroll in the state university system in Florida found that 77 percent of these students were eligible to continue in higher education after attending Miami-Dade Community College. It was also found that the proportion passing each College-Level Academic Skills Test (CLAST) subtest area declined as the number of students who needed preparatory help increased. It was concluded from this study that Miami-Dade Community College performs a valuable function in preparing students for continued study in the state university system. Another conclusion drawn from the study was that students who were initially eligible to enroll in the state university system were not handicapped by first attending the community college.

The issue of quality in two-year colleges and universities can be assessed from another perspective, that of the student who has been exposed to both experiences—the "reverse transfer." As the number of reverse transfers has increased over the past decade, this population has become a target for study. The Illinois Council on Articulation estimates that public two-year colleges receive as many transfers from four-year colleges as they send to those institutions. A study by Kuznik of these students (Losak, 1980) found that reverse transfers exhibited a greater level of satisfaction with the two-year college and that this satisfaction was attributed to more individual student attention at the community college, less competition, and a curriculum that was more relevant to vocational plans.

While the humanistic philosophies of open access and equal opportunity are indeed noble gestures, their cost must be justified. Since budget balancing and tax increases appear imminent, research must respond to the questions of success or failure that are generated by studies of students and programs.

The availability of programs on days and at times when adult students can attend provides options for traditional students and opportunities for nontraditional students who might not otherwise have the benefit of a college experience. Varied beginning and ending dates, flexible scheduling of classes, activities of varying lengths, and alternative teaching techniques and contexts are all examples of procedures that have proved valuable to open-access institutions. It has been proved that these techniques have all been successful for increasing numbers of students, but there is little research on any academic progress and student retention that may have resulted from these programs.

Community colleges have been forced to provide developmental services (compensatory and remedial classes) for students who had never considered going to college and were frequently not prepared for college-level work (Roueche, Baker, and Roueche, 1985). A national study conducted in 1977 by Roueche and Snow (Roueche, Baker, and Roueche, 1985) found that while colleges developed curricula for underprepared students, a majority of these institutions did not evaluate their efforts in programs and the success rates of those enrolled in regular courses after having taken developmental courses were rarely recorded or collected.

While many conventions have focused programs on basic skills and much has been written by practitioners, the evaluation of basic skills has not yet received serious institutional commitment. When evaluation data have been collected, they have rarely been sufficient to answer crucial questions about program effectiveness and instruction (Roueche, Baker, and Roueche, 1985).

Several states, including Virginia, Florida, and New Jersey, have compiled excellent statewide studies of basic-skills programs. One limitation of reporting across institutions is that it tends to cancel the uniqueness of programs at individual institutions. Research must be conducted at the institutional level, and quantitative data must be collected and analyzed. Local administrators and local governing boards and advisory committees can then base decisions on empirical evidence, rather than on subjective observations.

Employer Needs

There has been public disillusionment with higher education in recent years. Employers have often been disappointed by graduates who did not meet anticipated educational competencies, and graduates, involved in intense job competition, have been disenchanted with the benefits of earned degrees. Given the competition from foreign markets, the number of jobs has been steadily diminishing; employers have had large applicant pools, and applicants have had to compete on the basis of their abilities and educational qualifications. The elitist system of higher education no longer exists, because of social changes, the economic recession, new roles for minorities, and many other allied factors.

Wegmann (1985) notes some statistics that should cause much concern among educators. Today, one adult worker in four has a college degree, as compared to one in seven in 1970. From 1970 to 1980, the labor force grew by 31 percent; however, college graduates in the labor force increased by 85 percent. The number of jobs requiring college degrees did not increase at anywhere near that rate. While many graduates are not unemployed, they are underemployed. This trend is expected to continue throughout the present decade, with only 12 to 13 million jobs requiring workers with college degrees, and with 15 million graduates entering the labor market.

It will be up to educational institutions to determine the effects of students abandoning the liberal arts for courses in computer science, the technologies, and business. Some questions that must be answered through research concern the changing role of women (from the family to business), the long-term effects of the two-income family on child development, and the kinds of education people need to compete effectively in the international market.

Wegmann (1985) challenges colleges to examine within their own environment such questions as these:

1. What is the obligation of institutions to students who are admitted but do not graduate and who have to take the same jobs as students who graduate from high school?
2. Given the number of positions requiring advanced education, should institutions continue to accept as many students as they have in the past?
3. Should there be lower admission standards, as a means of avoiding faculty layoffs?

Wegmann emphasizes that on most campuses very little research is being done or instruction given on the labor market and its workings and on how to find employment.

Technology and the Information Age

As we enter the information age, the numbers of unskilled and semiskilled jobs are rapidly declining. There is an increasing number of jobs that require specific information skills, including reading, analyzing, defining, applying, interpreting, and communicating information. There are more jobs requiring information skills and fewer people who possess these skills (McCabe, 1984). Are we doing research that will enable our institutions to provide quality education to equip competent graduates with the skills needed by business and industry in the information age?

High technology will have an impact on institutions in two ways: Colleges will be forced to change curricula by adding new programs, and technology will change classroom activity and the ways instruction takes place. As the curriculum changes to accommodate the marketplace, we must confront the high cost of specialized facilities and sophisticated equipment. A second problem with high-technology curricula is their rapid equipment obsolescence (Koltai and Wolf, 1984). The impact of the initial costs and ongoing expenses of such programs, and the balance between liberal arts and vocational studies, are crucial areas for research.

In a period of rapid technological change, Fidler (1982) urges community colleges to become partners with business and industry in preparing a trained labor force. To do this, community colleges must keep pace with change and advance through leadership for industry development. Community colleges can serve as major resources for educational programs by providing employees with the skills necessary for the changing demands of business and industry.

The technological world is changing rapidly. The time lapse required to develop and introduce technologies that are increasingly sophisticated has dropped from a period of years to a period of months (Bush and Ames, 1984). High-technology hardware in the form of satellites, lasers, computers, robotics, and fiber optics is becoming increasingly less expensive. Fiber optic cables are being used by telephone companies to carry thousands of communications on a strand the size of a human hair. Lasers are being used with high-speed printers, which can quietly produce twelve pages of print per minute. Robotics are being introduced in some industrial and office situations. Computers that were once million-dollar investments can now be purchased by the average citizen. It is important for administrators to recognize the implications of the technological revolution. Instructional programs must incorporate technological advances in order to make students competitive in the job market.

Changing Times

Throughout their history, community colleges have developed their mission to serve changing conditions and needs in the external environment. Since the early part of this decade, there has been a focus on redefining the community college mission in response to changing roles, requirements, financial constraints, and changing public perceptions of community college education. This is in contrast to the 1970s, when the emphasis was on management systems, organizational development, and collective bargaining.

Alfred and Lowery (1984) conducted a study to determine the internally and externally focused issues of greatest concern to community colleges during the 1980s. The critical issues for institutional attention have focused on the concept of "putting America back to work." Cooperative partnerships, job retraining programs, needs assessment for industry, and models for cooperative education to improve linkages with business and industry are all means of:

- developing job retraining for workers displaced by the economic recession that began in 1975

- accommodating technological advances in business and industry by providing manpower training
- diversifying sources of revenue, as an alternative to relying on the decreased resources from state agencies and local tax districts
- improving basic skills in the natural and social sciences for underprepared learners.

The internal issues of greatest concern for community colleges during the late 1970s and early 1980s, as cited by Alfred and Lowery (1984), focused on academic programs, student services, institutional mission, changing technology, and new approaches to management. Faculty and staff concerns have focused on excellence in teaching, faculty retraining, relationships between full-time and part-time faculty, and faculty evaluation and compensation. Again, it must be stressed that while these are all topics of great administrative concern, few institutions can produce the kinds of research studies for local boards, state agencies, or legislatures, that can provide data analysis and interpretation of conditions within institutions.

Proactive Planning Through Research

As community colleges strive to serve the educational needs of their students and the community, they must offer broad-based curricula to accommodate a wide range of educational needs, while also providing high-quality learning experiences (Garrity, 1984). Curriculum changes within institutions are generally made without planning or research into the process. Institutional research can assist institutions in keeping pace with changes in community needs.

Pietack and Fenwick (1985) outline three areas of concern for community college occupational program administrators that can be supported by institutional research: rationales for new programs, reinforcement for existing programs, and recommendations for the elimination of programs that no longer meet the needs of the service area. Garrity (1984) outlines five areas for investigation to determine whether the curriculum is keeping pace with those it serves: What are the changes occurring in the job market? What are the changes in job demands as a result of technological advances? What needs are there for retraining and updating workers? Are students being advised of transfer requirements to four-year schools to ensure minimum loss of credits? What are the strengths and weaknesses of programs, as defined both by graduates who enter the job force and by those who transfer to four-year institutions?

How many institutions can say that research is being conducted in each of these areas to support organized and ongoing planning processes? Purga (1985) stresses that only with clear understanding of community needs can colleges allocate resources appropriately and effectively. With a majority of institutional resources being allocated to supporting curriculum offerings, program evaluation becomes essential for determining the value of existing programs. Needs assessment provides a new dimension for institutional research. Administrators must be able to incorporate information about the institution's clientele into operating strategies, delivery systems, and strategic planning to develop a communication network between the institution and those its serves.

Recommendations

There is an increasing need in postsecondary institutions, including community and junior colleges and technical-vocational institutions, to utilize applied institutional research. It is essential that institutions collect, analyze, and interpret data and distribute reports and other information in order to carry out the assessment of the need for educational programs and services and to evaluate the effectiveness of these programs and services for strategic planning. Institutional research can give direction by providing decision makers with accurate data concerning institutional operations.

Ironically, institutional research positions in community and technical colleges have steadily declined over the years, as the need for research and data analysis has increased. Mehallis (1981) stresses the need for institutions to establish research positions staffed by individuals who have doctorates in educational research and institutional research, who have been trained in the administration of higher education, including staffing, decision making, governance, facility construction, and research methodology. The caliber of these highly skilled individuals must exceed that of staff persons who have been assigned to work on institutional research.

In recent years, the position of institutional research director has been eliminated in many small institutions because of financial reasons, and in other institutions the position has been reclassified and renamed to include new or additional responsibilities. For example, in order to involve these people in professional associations, some state organizations and the Association for Institutional Research have either changed their names or expanded their association designations to include management, policy analysis, finance, and planning. In order to provide needed research on the issues discussed earlier, community colleges must establish goals and priorities and incorporate research in the decision-making process within the college.

While the large community colleges still maintain research and planning offices staffed by research professionals and support staff, many small institutions, in order to cut costs, have employed untrained, inexperienced people who can support the institution only through routine data collection and reporting while fulfilling other responsibilities, including teaching, computer operations, and student recruitment.

Coffey (1985) emphasizes the need for the assessment of external and internal environmental factors. Program evaluators must rely on statewide and local data to respond to very complex issues, including how to educate new and different student clienteles in addition to maintaining program quality and high academic standards and how to deal with the alteration of enrollment-driven funding formulas and increasing plant maintenance and equipment costs.

Bennett (1985) stresses that "those who pay for education must have reliable information about the quality of the institutions they are supporting." He urges states to promote access for qualified students and program excellence "by awarding a portion of their support to colleges and universities on the basis of reliable measures of institutional quality."

Edwards (1985) states that if "we do not address the question of compatibility between opportunity and excellence openly and convincingly, we may never fully realize our potential for what can be our greatest contribution to the future of this country." If accessibility is going to be community colleges' greatest contribution to higher education, then institutions must provide "more facts and less rhetoric."

Districts and institutions that have accurate assessments of their internal and external environment can make a dramatic difference in discussions with state agencies and legislatures. In responding to the questions raised in this discussion, researchers and institutions using research in their strategic planning processes will be in a better position to cope successfully with the complex and negative environmental factors in the next decade. Coffey (1985, p. 21) stresses that institutions using research "may have the ability not only to cope with change, but to be in a position to influence the very nature of that change."

References

Alfred, R. L. and Lowery, S. K. "Sign of the Times: AACJC Convention Focus." *Community and Junior College Journal*, 1984, 55 (1), 46–50.

Belcher, M., and Losak, J. *Providing Educational Opportunity for Students Who Were Initially Ineligible to Enroll in the State University System*. Miami: Office of Institutional Research, Miami–Dade Community College, 1985. 9 pp. (ED 256 453)

Bennett, W. "Self-Assessment by Colleges Urged." *Roanoke Times and World News*, November 1, 1985, p. 5.

Bush, R. W., and Ames, W. C. "Leadership and Technological Innovation." In R. L. Alfred, P. A. Elsner, R. J. LeCroy, and N. Armes (eds.), *Emerging Roles for Community College Leaders*. New Directions for Community Colleges, no. 46. San Francisco: Jossey-Bass, 1984.

Coffey, J. C. "Planning For Change: Assessing Internal and External Environmental Factors." *Community College Journal For Research and Planning*, 1985, 4 (2), 5–22.

Eaton, J. S. "Tapping Neglected Leadership Sources." In R. L. Alfred, P. A. Elsner, R. J. LeCroy, and N. Armes (eds.), *Emerging Roles for Community Col-*

lege Leaders. New Directions for Community Colleges, no. 46. San Francisco: Jossey-Bass, 1984.

Edwards, F. M. "Can Community Colleges Offer Opportunity and Excellence?" *Community, Technical and Junior College Journal,* 1985, *56* (2), 40-43.

Fidler, T. A. "Advancing Community College Impact Through Business and Industry." In R. L. Alfred (ed.), *Institutional Impacts on Campus, Community, and Business Constituencies.* New Directions for Community Colleges, no. 38. San Francisco: Jossey-Bass, 1982.

Garrity, R. J. "Curricula Excellence: The Role of the Advisory Committee." *Community and Junior College Journal,* 1984, *55* (2), 40-41.

Hall, T. M., and Reed, J. F. "Utilization of Student Information Systems." In M. Mehallis (ed.), *Improving Decision Making.* New Directions for Community Colleges, no. 35. San Francisco: Jossey-Bass, 1981.

Koltai, L., and Wolf, D. B. "A Reasonable Consensus." *Community and Junior College Journal,* 1984, *55* (1), 42-45.

Linthicum, D. S. "Does Community College Education Produce Changes in Students?" In R. L. Alfred (ed.), *Institutional Impacts on Campus, Community, and Business Constituencies.* New Directions for Community Colleges, no. 38. San Francisco: Jossey-Bass, 1982.

Losak, J. "Student Comparisons of Education Experiences at the Two Year College and the University: A Preliminary Study." *Community/Junior College Research Quarterly,* 1980, *4* (4), 362-363.

McCabe, R. H. "Dimensions of Change Confronting Institutional Leaders." In R. L. Alfred, P. A. Elsner, R. J. LeCroy, and N. Armes (eds.), *Emerging Roles for Community College Leaders.* New Directions for Community Colleges, no. 46. San Francisco: Jossey-Bass, 1984.

Mehallis, M. V. "Improving Decision Making Through Institutional Research." In M. Mehallis (ed.), *Improving Decision Making.* New Directions for Community Colleges, no. 35. San Francisco: Jossey-Bass, 1981.

Mortimer, K. P. "Text of New Report on Excellence in Undergraduate Education." *Chronicle of Higher Education,* October 24, 1984, p. 35.

Nielsen, R. M., and Polishook, I. "The Community College and Current Perspectives." *Chronicle of Higher Education,* January 20, 1982, p. 16.

Nielsen, R. M., and Polishook, I. "Academic Quality and Higher Education." *Chronicle of Higher Education,* November 21, 1984, p. 6.

Palmer, J. "How Is Quality Measured at the Community College?" *Community College Review,* 1983-84, *11* (3), 52-62.

Pietack, R. A., and Fenwick, D. "Back to Basics: What Department/Division Chairpersons Can Do to Enhance Occupational Program Services." *Community College Review,* 1985, *12* (4), 31-35.

Purga, A. "The President's Forum—Needs Assessment and Institutional Vitality." *Community College Journal for Research and Planning,* 1985, *4* (2), 1-4.

Roueche, J. E., Baker, G. A., III, and Roueche, S. D. "Access with Excellence: Toward Academic Success in College." *Community College Review,* 1985, *12,* (4), 5-8.

Stevenson, M. R., and Walleri, R. D. "Financial Decision Making in a Period of Retrenchment." In M. Mehallis (ed.), *Improving Decision Making.* New Directions for Community Colleges, no. 35. San Francisco: Jossey-Bass, 1981.

Thompson, C. P. "Maintaining Quality with Open Access." *Community College Review,* 1985, *12* (4), 10-14.

Wegmann, R. D. "Looking for Work in a New Economy." *Change,* 1985, *17* (4), 41-47.

Edith H. Carter is editor of the Journal of the National Council of Research and Planning *and a former institutional research director at a community college.*

Additional resources abstracted from the Educational Resources Information Center (ERIC) provide further information on institutional research.

Sources and Information: Institutional Research at the Community College

Diane Zwemer

This chapter presents an annotated bibliography of selected ERIC documents and journal articles on community college institutional research, covering the years 1981 through 1986. The entries in the bibliography are divided into three sections. Part one lists works providing general discussions of problems, practices, and priorities in institutional research, focusing primarily on needs assessment, program evaluation, and the effective use of data gathered in institutional research efforts. Part two lists the few recent works covering the roles and activities of institutional research offices. Part three presents manuals and other documents delineating guidelines to be followed in conducting various research studies, including student follow-ups, telephone surveys, needs assessments, and economic-impact analyses. The bibliography does not include institutional research reports from individual community colleges. Such reports, many of which contain survey instruments and other research tools, may be located through searches of ERIC's *Resources in Education.*

Most of the items cited in this bibliography are ERIC documents and are therefore marked with ED numbers. These documents can be viewed on microfiche at more than 750 libraries across the country or ordered at cost of reproduction and mailing from the ERIC Document Reproduction Service (EDRS) in Alexandria, Virginia. Those items not marked with ED numbers are journal articles and must be obtained through regular library channels. For an EDRS order form and a list of the libraries in your state that have ERIC microfiche collections, contact the ERIC Clearinghouse for Junior Colleges, 8118 Math-Sciences Building, UCLA, 405 Hilgard, Los Angeles, CA 90024.

Problems, Practices, and Priorities in Institutional Research

Blong, J. T., and Purga, A. J. "Institutional Research: A Critical Component of Sound Financial Planning." In D. F. Campbell (ed.), *Strengthening Financial Management*. New Directions for Community Colleges, no. 50. San Francisco: Jossey-Bass, 1985. 135 pp. (ED 258 654)

Points out that community college program evaluation has not focused on the effectiveness of program offerings. Argues that community colleges must be able to incorporate information about themselves and their clientele into delivery systems, operational strategies, and strategic planning. Stresses that program evaluation involves an analysis of both efficiency and effectiveness and outlines steps for a successful needs assessment. Underscores the importance of program evaluation in institutional planning and of needs assessment as a vital communication process between the college and its service areas.

California Community Colleges. *Measuring Community College Learner Outcomes: State-of-the-Art. Improving Community College Evaluation and Planning: Project Working Paper Number Ten*. Sacramento: Office of the Chancellor, California Community Colleges; Aptos, Calif.: Accrediting Commission for Community and Junior Colleges, Western Association of Schools and Colleges, 1982. 91 pp. (ED 250 041)

Discusses the outcomes approach to evaluation in higher education and describes current projects utilizing outcomes measures in community colleges. Examines three types of learner outcomes: concrete learner outcomes, such as transfer or degree attainment; abstract learner outcomes, such as cognitive and affective development; and social outcomes, such as benefits to the local community. Concludes with a review of the ways in which outcomes evaluation has been put to use in postsecondary education, focusing on standardized testing and measurement of outcomes. Attempts to refine the concept of outcomes measurement and the use of outcomes measurement in management and college funding.

Cross, K. P. "The State of the Art in Needs Assessments." *Community/Junior College Quarterly of Research and Practice*, 1983, 7 (3), 195-206.

Draws upon forty major research studies to examine the status of needs-assessment studies at community colleges. Discusses (1) who conducts needs assessments and why, (2) common faults in needs assessments, (3) what has been learned from these studies, and (4) what needs assessments cannot do. Emphasizes that many needs assessments merely confirm what is already known (such as the axiom that the more education people have, the more likely they are to participate in formal educational activities).

Gold, B. K. *Institutional Research at Los Angeles City College: A Thirty-Five-Year Perspective.* Los Angeles: Los Angeles City College, 1982. 21 pp. (ED 215 724)

Provides a thirty-five-year perspective on institutional research at Los Angeles City College. Focuses on seven five-year periods, highlighting research activities and findings relevant to each. Notes that certain research concerns were common to most periods, but that priorities for research often change with time. Demonstrates how changing societal conditions require institutional researchers to shift the focus of their attention as the years go by.

Gollattscheck, J. F. "Assessing Social and Economic Benefits to the Community." In R. L. Alfred (ed.), *Institutional Impacts on Campus, Community, and Business Constituencies.* New Directions for Community Colleges, no. 38. San Francisco: Jossey-Bass, 1982. 130 pp. (ED 217 944)

Presents three case studies showing how impact studies can be conducted in a constantly changing community environment. Describes the impact of a community college as direct or indirect, depending on relationships between resources and outcomes. Recommends planned, coordinated assessment programs as tools for decision makers.

Kennedy, W. R. "Strategic Planning and Program Evaluation in the Community College." Paper presented at the annual meeting of the American Educational Research Association, Los Angeles, April 13-17, 1981. 17 pp. (ED 202 506)

Notes the increased need to evaluate community college programs on the basis of long-term strategic information relating to projected market forces, such as the future economic health of the community or expectations for future state funding. Argues that tactical program-evaluation data relating to past or current enrollment and funding may serve the needs of external funding agencies, but that such data are of little value to institutional planners. Suggests the use of a strategic mode that evaluates programs on the basis of their contributions to long-term institutional goals.

Losak, J., and Morris, C. *Integrating Research into Decision Making: Providing Examples for an Informal Action Research Model. Research Report No. 83-24.* Miami, Fla.: Office of Institutional Research, Miami-Dade Community College, 1983, 17 pp. (ED 239 674)

Suggests that the informal action research model may increase the utilization of institutional research data by decision makers. Notes that informal action researchers must (1) have knowledge of pressing issues, (2) use informal communication channels, (3) anticipate information needs, (4) provide concise and timely data, and (5) use multiple channels for disseminating data. Illustrates the use of informal action research at Miami-Dade Community College.

Luna, C. L. "A Study of Community College Needs Assessment Practices and Outcomes: Institutional and Contextual Predictors." Paper presented at the annual meeting of the American Educational Research Association, Los Angeles, April 13-17, 1981. 20 pp. (ED 203 947)

Draws upon a survey of 1,127 public two-year colleges to examine the extent to which the colleges were involved in formalized needs-assessment projects from 1976 to 1979, to identify the strategies used in planning and conducting these studies, and to determine the ways in which the colleges benefited from this research. Compares findings with data from the Higher Education General Information Surveys to determine (1) the correlation of involvement in needs assessment projects with institutional and contextual characteristics, such as institutional sizes; and (2) the correlations between these characteristics and the reported outcomes of needs assessments. Summarizes major findings and discusses areas for further study.

Mehallis, M. (ed.). *Improving Decision Making*. New Directions for Community Colleges, no. 35. San Francisco: Jossey-Bass, 1981. 124 pp. (ED 207 650)

Provides nine essays focusing on the importance of accurate and timely information for effective decision making. Includes articles on (1) ways to improve statewide research; (2) strategies for using research to influence policy making; (3) research as a tool in the development of master plans; (4) information-resource management; (5) the use of student data in planning; (6) the utilization of student information systems; (7) guidelines for financial decision making in a period of retrenchment; and (8) improved decision making through institutional research. Concludes with a review of relevant ERIC documents.

Mehallis, M. V. *Responding to Community Needs Through Community Follow-Up. Junior College Resource Review*. Los Angeles, Calif.: ERIC Clearinghouse for Junior Colleges, 1981. 6 pp. (ED 202 564)

Examines the utilization of community needs-assessment data in program planning and evaluation efforts at community colleges, noting that few such studies have actually led to substantial program change. Discusses the importance of identifying the needs of subgroups within a community and considers the application of needs assessment findings to institutional marketing. Summarizes problems in needs-assessment practices, including vague definitions of *need* and *community*, poor data-collection and -interpretation techniques, and continual reliance on data-gathering systems that meet legislatively mandated reporting requirements rather than institutional needs.

Parson, S. R. "Impact Assessment: What Have You Done for Us Lately?" *Community Services Catalyst,* 1983, *13* (2), 17-19.

Urges more attempts to measure the community impacts of continuing education and community service programs. Calls for a review of priorities in these areas and for an emphasis on programs that have measurable community impacts. Suggests research on costs, funding sources, participant and recipient identification, changes within the community, and program effects on individuals.

Richardson, R. C., Jr. "Setting an Agenda for Research on the Community College." *Community College Review,* 1985, *13* (2), 4-9.

Summarizes several significant research studies conducted since 1978 that have focused on community colleges. Offers an agenda for future research, covering student objectives and outcomes, administrative decision making, and faculty-administrator relationships. Identifies several research issues that are fundamental in today's competitive educational environment, including the current status of the community college professoriate, governance structures, institutional mission, and finance.

Wattenbarger, J. L. "Research as a Basis for Improving the Community College." *Community College Review,* 1983, *10* (4), 58-62.

Points out some omissions in the body of community college institutional research and offers topics for research as a basis for improvement. Suggests that increased attention be paid to mission, philosophical commitments, institutional management and operations, faculty role, student needs, academic planning, community services, and lifelong education.

Wright, T. *Who Uses Institutional Research and Why? Research Report No. 85-22.* Miami, Fla.: Office of Institutional Research, Miami-Dade Community College, 1985. 19 pp. (ED 267 879)

Summarizes a survey conducted at Miami-Dade Community College to assess the usefulness of providing faculty and administrators with institutional research information in the form of abstracts and/or full research reports. Surveys chairpersons, administrators, faculty senate presidents, and a sample of administrative/professional staff members on (1) the categories of reports used in decision making, (2) how soon the abstracts or reports are read after they are received, (3) whether college personnel are interested in receiving reports on research outside their areas of responsibility, and (4) preferred formats for receiving information.

The Institutional Research Office

Chalker, C. D. "Presidents' Perceptions of the Role of Institutional Research in Rural Junior Colleges in the Southeast." Paper presented at the annual meeting of the Southeastern Association for Community College Research, Orlando, Fla., July 20-22, 1981. 15 pp. (ED 206 336)

Surveys the presidents at 135 rural community colleges in the Southeast to determine their perceptions of the role and activities of the office of institutional research. Notes that many schools have inadequate institutional research programs because of limited funding, lack of administrative emphasis, and lack of full-time directors.

Knapp, M. S. *Summary of Findings: A Study of Institutional Research and Planning Unit Development in California Community Colleges.* Sacramento: California Community and Junior College Association, 1981. 8 pp. (ED 203 921)

Reports the findings of a 1979 study conducted to (1) determine the organizational factors that influence the growth or decline of community college research, evaluation, and planning—or REP—units and (2) to assess the impact of Proposition 13 (a tax-limitation measure) on these units. Reveals that most REP units were viewed as nonessential; and that they were more likely to be funded if they provided information on topics of pressing organizational concern, rather than information for external reporting requirements.

Ladwig, D. J. "All in the Family: An Alternative Approach to Applied Research." *Community and Junior College Journal*, 1985, 56 (1), 34-36.

Notes that staff members at Lakeshore Technical Institute (Wisconsin) have been encouraged to enroll in higher education programs and undertake applied institutional research projects that help solve institutional problems. Provides examples of research projects conducted by staff members, including the investigation of a quality-circle model for decision making. Suggests that a cadre of staff members skilled in applied research techniques may prove a viable alternative to an institutional research department.

Wilcox, S. A. "Evaluation of the Research Function in a Large Community College District." Paper presented at the annual meeting of the California Educational Research Association, Sacramento, November 17-18, 1982. 10 pp. (ED 229 089)

Examines research activities undertaken in the Los Angeles Community College District. Identifies staff and fiscal resources allocated to research; activities in which researchers are involved; amount of time devoted to each activity; and areas that researchers feel should be expanded or deleted. Reveals that the largest proportion of research time is spent on identifying trends, conducting student follow-up studies, and evaluating programs.

Guidelines and Procedures

Armes, N., Griffith, J. S., and Trout, L. (eds.). *Guidelines for the Development of Computerized Student Information Systems.* Laguna Hills, Calif.: League for Innovation in the Community College, 1984. 35 pp. (ED 250 021)

Outlines guidelines to be followed in developing computerized student-information systems. Examines the components of student information systems with respect to admissions, assessment and counseling, registration, academic-alert monitoring, degree audit, transfer requirements, and student follow-up. Lists the reports that may be part of each component and the data elements required to generate those reports. Concludes with recommendations for developing and using computer-based information systems.

Baldwin, A. *Placement and Follow-Up Summary Manual: Miami–Dade Community College.* Miami, Fla.: Office of Institutional Research, Miami–Dade Community College, 1985. 50 pp. (ED 269 110)

Provides information on the accountability reports prepared by Miami–Dade Community College for use at the federal, state, and local levels. Explains data-collection activities in seven areas: (1) program enrollments and completions, (2) preprogram admittance, (3) supplemental, special needs, and apprenticeship course enrollments, (4) developmental and community instructional service enrollments, (5) the feedback system to produce reports on the status of community college graduates, (6) surveys of former students, and (7) other activities, such as surveys of campus nurses and handicap coordinators. Also explains procedures used in processing collected data, checking for data accuracy and integrity, and creating master and work files.

Butler, D. G. *Busy Signal: Techniques and Methods Used for Planning and Executing the 1980 Community Telephone Survey. Coast Community Colleges Community Telephone Survey, 1980: Report Number 8.* Costa Mesa, Calif.: Coast Community College District, 1981. 48 pp. (ED 215 735)

Provides information on the procedures and instruments used by the Coast Community College District (California) to conduct a telephone survey in 1980. Presents the research design for the project and considers models and procedures of data collection. Describes the key elements of data analysis and provides information on ways to report survey results. Includes the survey instrument and instructions for interviewers.

California Community Colleges. *Census Users Manual. Improving Community College Evaluation and Planning.* Sacramento: Office of the

Chancellor, California Community Colleges; Aptos, Calif.: Accrediting Commission for Community and Junior Colleges, Western Association of Schools and Colleges, 1983. 64 pp. (ED 250 045)

Explains how colleges can use census data to assess the characteristics and educational requirements of individuals within their service areas. Describes how and where to obtain census data, noting the types of data that are available and the kinds of district data aggregations that can be produced. Also examines ways census data can be used, focusing on applications in college planning, on the establishment or modification of state priorities, and on the accreditation process.

California Community Colleges. *College Planning: Strategies for Assessing the Environment. Improving Community College Evaluation and Planning.* Sacramento: Office of the Chancellor, California Community Colleges; Aptos, Calif.: Accrediting Commission for Community and Junior Colleges, Western Association of Schools and Colleges, 1983. 73 pp. (ED 250 044)

Provides information and guidance for conducting strategic planning at community colleges. Discusses strategies for assessing the external environment and describes how to synthesize large amounts of complex information on environmental trends. Also summarizes a series of workshops on planning and evaluation, demonstrating ways of using institutional teams to gather and interpret information for strategic plans.

California Community Colleges. *Learner Outcomes Handbook. Improving Community Colleges Evaluation and Planning.* Sacramento: Office of the Chancellor, California Community Colleges; Aptos, Calif.: Accrediting Commission for Community and Junior Colleges, Western Association of Schools and Colleges, 1984. 71 pp. (ED 250 047)

Describes three procedures for documenting student learning: direct assessment through testing; the review of existing college records; and follow-up surveys. Also explores different uses of learner-outcomes data and provides information on sampling theory.

Grand Rapids Junior College. *MANAGER (Michigan Analysis Network and General Evaluation Report) Handbook.* Grand Rapids, Mich.: Office of Curriculum Planning and Evaluation, Grand Rapids Junior College, 1982. 191 pp. (ED 234 833)

Describes the Michigan Analysis Network and General Evaluation Report (MANAGER), a six-step process for collecting, analyzing, synthesizing, and interpreting data to be used in self-evaluations of occupational programs. Details procedures used in (1) collecting and formatting evaluation data, (2) reviewing the formatted data against a set of standards, (3) generating questions and concerns from the review, (4) obtaining answers to these questions from key personnel, (5) selecting alternative actions to address major concerns, and (6) monitoring implemented actions. Includes extensive appendixes that provide sample forms and field-test results.

Hopson, C. S., Montgomery, M. D., Aspiazu, G., and Lagasse, E. M. "The Needs Assessment as a Planning Tool for the 1980s." Paper presented at the annual convention of the American Association of Community and Junior Colleges, New Orleans, April 24-27, 1983. 31 pp. (ED 231 433)

Draws upon the experiences of Delgado Community College (Louisiana) to examine the application of needs assessments to institutional planning. Includes discussions of (1) the administrative decisions to be made before beginning a needs assessment (including those related to budgeting and staffing), (2) step-by-step procedures for collecting and analyzing data in needs-assessment studies, (3) the role of an advisory committee in the needs-assessment process, and (4) how needs-assessment results are used in discontinuing, modifying, and adding programs.

Kinnick, M. K. (ed.). *Oregon Community College Economic Impact Study: A Guidebook*. Gresham, Ore.: Office of Research, Mount Hood Community College, 1982. 84 pp. (ED 222 233)

Outlines the procedures used in conducting a study of the economic impact of Oregon's community colleges. Includes discussions of (1) the purpose, focus, and scope of the Oregon study; (2) key steps in the early planning stages of the study; (3) factors impeding the progress of the study; (4) procedures in data collection and processing; and (5) the dissemination of study findings through press releases, in-house publications, and reports to college boards. Serves as a step-by-step guide to conducting economic impact studies.

Michigan State Department of Education. *MiSIS (Michigan Student Information System) Procedures Manual*. Lansing: Higher Education Management Services, Michigan State Department of Education, 1979. 113 pp. (ED 234 832)

Provides guidelines to be followed in collecting data for the Michigan Student Information System (MiSIS), the student-flow component of a comprehensive statewide system for evaluating occupational education. Includes step-by-step procedures for collecting and analyzing data in each of six MiSIS subsystems: (1) student educational intent, (2) nonreturning student follow-up, (3) withdrawal follow-up, (4) graduate follow-up, (5) employer follow-up, and (6) continuing education follow-up. Also describes the relationship between MiSIS and the Vocational Education Data System.

Morris, W., Gold, B. K., and McGillicuddy, S. *Student Accountability Model (SAM) Operations Manual*. Sacramento: Office of the Chancellor,

California Community Colleges; Los Angeles: Los Angeles Community College District, 1981. 98 pp. (ED 207 644)

Outlines procedures used in California's Student Accountability Model (SAM), a system designed to improve occupational student follow-up. Details two SAM components: (1) the student accounting component, which includes procedures for classifying courses, identifying student majors, and obtaining unduplicated enrollment counts; and (2) the student follow-up component, which recommends procedures for obtaining information about students who have left college. Includes sample survey instruments and a discussion of sampling techniques for follow-up research.

Parsons, M. H. "Where Do We Go From Here? The Use of the Market Analysis Survey in Needs Assessment and Program Development." Paper presented at the National Conference on Needs Assessment, Blacksburg, Va., May 11, 1982. 16 pp. (ED 217 909)

Argues that market analysis can be a mechanism for making needs assessment functional and for focusing program development on community constituencies that need to be served. Lists four steps in conducting successful market analyses: identifying the institutions that have impacts on the markets served; determining which market data already exist; designing, testing, and implementing the market analysis survey and then discussing its results with participating groups; and conducting a follow-up survey. Highlights the benefits of market analysis by noting its use at Hagerstown Junior College (Maryland) in developing a health care degree program and streamlining a merchandising program.

Sheldon, M. S. *Pattern for Vocational Follow-Up.* Woodland Hills, Calif.: Los Angeles Pierce College, 1981. 25 pp. (ED 206 367)

Outlines the prototypical procedures followed in vocational follow-up studies and describes their implementation in the evaluation of the electronics, computer science, and manufacturing programs at Los Angeles Pierce College. Reviews problems in sampling as well as data-collection procedures involving a highly structured telephone interview to determine student characteristics as well as students' assessments of their own college experiences. Concludes with recommendations regarding the purpose and value of vocational follow-up at the institutional and state levels.

Wallhaus, P., and Lach, I. J. *Handbook for Conducting a Study of the Economic Impact of a Community College.* Springfield: Illinois Community College Board, 1981. 43 pp. (ED 237 137)

Examines procedures to be followed in conducting community college economic-impact studies and explains models for assessing seven types of economic impacts: (1) college-related local business volume, (2) value of local business property committed to college-related business, (3) expansion of local banks' credit base, (4) college-related revenues received by local governments, (5) operating costs of government-provided services applicable to college-related influences, (6) number of local jobs attributable to the presence of the college, and (7) personal income of local individuals from college-related jobs and business activities. Also includes questionnaires used in economic-impact studies and explains the concept and use of economic multipliers.

Diane Zwemer is the user services librarian at the ERIC Clearinghouse for Junior Colleges, University of California at Los Angeles.

Index

A

Access, and quality, 88-90
Accreditation, and effectiveness, 50
Alfred, R. L., 92-93, 95
American Association of Community and Junior Colleges, 37, 46, 50
American Association of State Colleges and Universities, 70, 72
American Council on Education, 49, 59
Ames, W. C., 92, 95
Anderson, R. A., 36, 46
Armes, N., 105
Aspiazu, G., 107
Assessment, development of, and strategic management, 41-43
Association for Institutional Research, 94
Association of American Colleges, 49, 60

B

Baker, G., 76, 83, 90, 96
Baldwin, A., 105
Barnard, C., 51, 60
Basonic, N., 4, 5, 10
Belcher, M. J., 7, 8, 10, 79, 82, 89, 95
Bennett, W., 95
Bers, T., 4, 10-11
Blong, J. T., 100
Bogen, G. K., 53, 55, 60
Boggs, G., 4, 11
Borst, P., 4, 11
Boyer, E. L., 45, 46
Boylan, H., 3, 4, 5, 11
Bray, D., 39, 46
Broward Community College, leadership, marketing, and research at, 79, 80
Bryant, P. S., 28, 32
Bush, R. W., 92, 95
Butler, D. G., 105

C

California, student data needs in, 15
California Community Colleges, 100, 105-106
Cameron, K., 55, 56, 60
Career assessment center, and strategic management, 42
Carnegie Foundation for the Advancement of Teaching, 45
Carter, E. H., 1, 85, 97
Chalker, C. D., 104
Change, challenges of, 85-96
Coffey, J. C., 95
Cohen, E. L., 39, 47
Coker, R., 39, 47
College Board, 77
College-Level Academic Skills Test (CLAST), 7, 8, 9, 10, 78-79, 89
College preparatory program: analysis of research on, 3-12; background on, 3-4; and course enrollment, 6-8; literature review on, 4; longitudinal research on, 8-9; and placement test scores, 5-6; summary on, 9-10
Colorado Commission of Higher Education, 45
Colorado Consortium of Two-Year Community/Junior Colleges, 45
Commission for the Review of the Master Plan for Higher Education, 15
Community, and leadership, marketing, and research, 80-81
Community colleges: access and quality in, 88-90; analysis of changes for, 85-96; background on, 85-96; and employer needs, 90-91; and external environment changes, 92-93; growth period for, 86-88; and proactive planning, 93; recommendations for, 94-95; and technology, 91-92
Computer-Based Training Conference and Exposition, 69
Control Data, 69
Cordrey, L., 4, 11
Cross, K. P., 100-101
Curriculum, renewal of, and strategic management, 40-41

111

D

Davis, D., 77, 82
Decision making: and enrollment/ marketing research, 29-31; in strategic management, 37-38
Demographic trends: and external environment, 63; and leadership, 76
Duke, D. L., 38, 47

E

Eaton, J. S., 86, 95-96
Economic trends, and external environment, 64-65
Edlin, W., 66, 72
Edwards, F. M., 95, 96
Effectiveness: assessment of, 49-60; conclusion on, 59; criteria of, 54, 55-57; and data collection and use, 58-59; defining, 51-54; emphasis on, 49-51; institutional research role in, 54-59; and mission and goals, 52-53, 54-55; and outcomes data base, 57-58; and planning process, 53-54
Elfrey, P., 70, 72
Employers, needs of, 90-91
Enrollment/marketing research: analysis of, 27-33; background on, 28-30; and class offerings, 30-31; data elements for, 28-30; and decision making, 29-31; evaluation of, 31-32; literature review on, 27-28; and marketing, 29-30; summary on, 32
Environment scanning, 63
Eurich, N. P., 45, 47, 66, 72
Ewell, P., 5, 58, 60
External environment: assessment of, 61-73; background on, 61-62; changes in, 92-93; conclusions on, 71-72; and demographic trends, 63; and economic trends, 64-65; and information technologies, 69-70; and policy issues, 71-72; and political change, 65-66; and social indicators, 63-64; and strategic planning and management, 62; techniques for assessing, 62-71; and technological advances, 66-68; and value shifts, 70-71; and workplace changes, 68-69

F

Fadale, L., 4, 11
Fenske, R. H., 54-55, 60
Fenwick, D., 93, 96
Fidler, T. A., 92, 96
Fincher, C., 54, 57, 60
Finegold, S. N., 69, 72
Fisher, J. L., 35, 47
Florida: basic-skills programs in, 89, 90; exit-level testing in, 7, 78
Fox, K., 27, 32

G

Garrity, R. J., 93, 96
Gash, P., 4, 11
Gold, B. K., 101, 107-108
Gollatscheck, J. F., 72, 101
Grand Rapids Junior College, 106-107
Griffith, J. S., 105
Groff, W. H., 1, 61, 62, 72, 73

H

Hall, T. M., 88, 96
Harlacher, E. L., 72
Harrower, G., Jr., 43, 47
Hawley, W. D., 36, 47
Helms, W. C., 69, 72
Hopson, C. S., 107

I

Idaho, demographic increase in, 63
Illinois, University of, and PLATO, 69
Illinois Council on Articulation, 89
Image improvement, and strategic management, 43-44
Information, technologies for, 69-70, 91-92
Institutional research: and assessment of effectiveness, 49-60; and challenge of change, 85-96; on college preparatory program, 3-12; directions for, 81; extent of, 37; on external environment, 61-73; guidelines for, 105-109; leadership and marketing integrated with, 75-83; on marketing, 27-33; on nontraditional

programs, 3–12; offices for, 104–105; for planning, 13–25; and proactive planning, 93; problems, practices, and priorities in, 100–104; recommendations on, 94–95; sources and information on, 99–109; and strategic management, 35–48

J

Johnson, B., 4, 11
Joint Economic Committee of the Congress of the United States, 66–67, 72
Jones, D. P., 58, 60
Jones, R. F., 28, 32
Jones, S. W., 39, 47
Joseph, N., 4, 11

K

Kegg, R., 67, 72
Keller, A., 35–36, 37, 39, 47
Keller, L. J., 45, 47
Kelly, J. T., 1, 75, 83
Kennedy, W. R., 101
Kinnick, M. K., 107
Knapp, M. S., 104
Koltai, L., 92, 96
Kotler, P., 27, 32
Kulik, C., 4, 11
Kulik, J., 4, 11
Kuznik, 89

L

Lach, I. J., 108–109
Ladwig, D. J., 104
Lagasse, E. M., 107
Law, W. D., Jr., 57, 60
Lawrence, B., 51, 53, 60
Leadership: analysis of integrating with marketing and research, 75–83; background on, 75–76; and community attitudes, 80–81; conclusion on, 81–82; and data configurations, 76–79; and demographics, 76; and student satisfaction, 79–80
Levin, H. M., 68, 73
Levitz, R., 39, 47
Linthicum, D. S., 86, 96
Longitudinal data, research using, 8–9

Losak, J., 1, 2, 3, 5, 6, 7, 8, 11, 12, 28, 32, 39, 47, 89, 95, 96, 101–102
Lowery, S. K., 92–93, 95
Lukenbill, J., 77, 82
Luna, C. L., 102
Lutkus, A., 4, 5, 11

M

McCabe, R., 77, 81, 82, 83, 91, 96
McClain, C. J., 57, 60
McClenney, B. N., 52, 57, 60
McGillicuddy, S., 107–108
Management, student questionnaires for, 13–25. *See also* Strategic management
Manufacturing, technological advances in, 67
Market analysis, 63
Marketing: decision making in, 29–30; institutional research on, 27–33; leadership and research integrated with, 75–83. *See also* Enrollment/marketing research
Maxwell, M., 3, 11
Mehallis, M. V., 28, 33, 80, 94, 96, 102–103
Miami-Dade Community College: and access, 89; college preparatory analysis at, 3–10; leadership, marketing, and research at, 76–79, 81
Michigan State Department of Education, 107
Miller, C., 4, 11
Mission and goals, and effectiveness, 52–53, 54–55
Montgomery, M. D., 107
Moody, H. G., 66, 73
Moore, K. M., 1, 49, 60
Morris, C., 1, 3, 5, 6, 8, 11, 12, 28, 32, 39, 47, 101–102
Morris, W., 107–108
Mortimer, K. P., 87–88, 96
Moss, J., 1, 13, 25
Myran, G. A., 35, 37, 47

N

National Center for Higher Education Management Systems, 56
National Center for Student Retention, 44

National Commission on Excellence in Education, 36, 47, 49, 60
National Institute of Education, 45, 47, 49, 60, 87
Needs assessment, 63
New Jersey, basic-skills programs in, 90
New York, developmental program success criteria study in, 4-5
Newman, F., 45, 47
Nielsen, R. M., 86-87, 88, 96
Nontraditional programs, institutional research on, 3-12

O

Ohio, economic trends in, 64
Oklahoma City Community College, enrollment research at, 27, 29-32
Otto, A. M., 1, 75, 83

P

Palmer, J., 88-89, 96
Parson, S. R., 103
Parsons, M. H., 108
Persistence, and college preparatory programs, 6, 7, 8-9, 10
Peters, T., 79, 83
Pietack, R. A., 93, 96
Placement test scores, research using, 5-6
Planning: and effectiveness, 53-54; institutional research for, 13-25; proactive, 93
Polishook, I., 86-87, 88, 96
Political trends, in external environment, 65-66
Programmed Logic for Automatic-Teaching Operations (PLATO), 69
Pueblo Community College, strategic management at, 38-44
Purga, A. J., 93, 96, 100

Q

Quality, and access, 88-90

R

Rankin, G., 1, 27, 33
Readability, and curriculum renewal, 41

Reed, J. F., 88, 96
Reed, J. G., 39, 47
Remediation, development of, and strategic management, 41-43. *See also* College preparatory program
Retention, and strategic management, 38-44
Rice, G., 28, 33
Richardson, R. C., Jr., 103
Roberts, E., 72
Romney, L. C., 53, 55, 60
Roueche, J. E., 4, 12, 76, 82, 83, 90, 96
Roueche, S. D., 90, 96
Rounds, J. C., 39, 47
Rumberger, R. W., 68, 73
Rumelt, R. P., 37, 47

S

San Francisco Community College District, student information questionnaire of 14-25
Sheldon, M. S., 108
Shwalb, B., 4, 11
Snow, J. J., 90
Social indicators, in external environment, 63-64
Southern Association of Colleges and Schools, 50, 60
Southern Colorado, University of, institutional split at, 38
Southern Regional Education Board, 3, 12, 49-50, 60
Stevenson, M. R., 85, 96
Stopouts, and enrollment/marketing research, 32
Strategic management: analysis of, 35-48; for assessment and remediation, 41-43; case study of, 38-44; conclusion on, 46; and curriculum renewal, 40-41; decision making in, 37-38; and external environment, 62; and image improvement, 43-44; and learning process, 45-46; need for, 35-37; research results for 44-45
Student information questionnaire (SIQ): administration of, 23-24; analysis of, 13-25; background of, 14-15; benefits of, 22; conclusion on, 25; costs of, 25; and data needs, 15-16; design of, 22-23; development of, 16-17; examples of, 18-19;

and facilities location, 20-21; methodology for, 2-25; need for, 13-14, 15-16; processing, 24; for program planning and evaluation, 21-22; reporting from, 24-25; for student services, 21; time line for, 25; for transportation and parking facilities, 17, 20; uses of, 17-22
Students, satisfaction of, 79-80. *See also* Persistence; Retention
Suter, M., 4, 12

T

Technology: advances in, 66-68; and external environment, 61-73, 91-92
Texas, University of, study by, 76
Thompson, C. P., 88, 89, 96
Trend analysis, 63
Trout, L., 105

U

Utah, demographic increase in, 63

V

Vaden, S., 4, 12

Values, shifts of, 70-71
Virginia, basic-skills programs in, 90

W

Walleri, R. D., 85, 96
Wallhaus, P., 108-109
Watcke, R. R., 66, 73
Waterman, R., 79, 83
Wattenbarger, J. L., 103
Wegmann, R. D., 90-91, 96
Whited, C., 78, 83
Wilcox, S. A., 104-105
Wilson, M., 4, 12
Winter, G., 4, 11
Wolf, D. B., 92, 96
Workplace, changes in, 68-69
Wright, T., 103
Wygal, B. R., 72
Wyoming, demographic increase in, 63

Z

Zeiss, P. A., 1, 35, 48
Zwemer, D., 2, 99, 109

STATEMENT OF OWNERSHIP, MANAGEMENT AND CIRCULATION

1A. TITLE OF PUBLICATION: New Directions for Community Colleges
1B. PUBLICATION NO.: 1 2 1 7 1 0
2. DATE OF FILING: 9/26/96
3. FREQUENCY OF ISSUE: Quarterly
3A. NO. OF ISSUES PUBLISHED ANNUALLY: 4
3B. ANNUAL SUBSCRIPTION PRICE: $30 indv/$40 inst

4. COMPLETE MAILING ADDRESS OF KNOWN OFFICE OF PUBLICATION: 433 California St., San Francisco (SF County), CA 94104

5. COMPLETE MAILING ADDRESS OF THE HEADQUARTERS OF GENERAL BUSINESS OFFICES OF THE PUBLISHER: 433 California St., San Francisco (SF County), CA 94104

6. FULL NAMES AND COMPLETE MAILING ADDRESS OF PUBLISHER, EDITOR, AND MANAGING EDITOR

PUBLISHER: Jossey-Bass Inc., Publishers, 433 California St., San Francisco, CA 94104

EDITOR: Arthur Cohen, ERIC, 8118 Library Sciences Bldg., UCLA, Los Angeles, CA 90024

MANAGING EDITOR: Allen Jossey-Bass, Jossey-Bass Publishers, 433 California St., SF, CA 94104

7. OWNER:

FULL NAME	COMPLETE MAILING ADDRESS
Jossey-Bass Inc., Publishers	433 California St., S.F., CA 94104

For names and addresses of stockholders, see attached list.

8. KNOWN BONDHOLDERS, MORTGAGEES, AND OTHER SECURITY HOLDERS OWNING OR HOLDING 1 PERCENT OR MORE OF TOTAL AMOUNT OF BONDS, MORTGAGES OR OTHER SECURITIES:

FULL NAME	COMPLETE MAILING ADDRESS
Same as #7	

10. EXTENT AND NATURE OF CIRCULATION

	AVERAGE NO. COPIES EACH ISSUE DURING PRECEDING 12 MONTHS	ACTUAL NO. COPIES OF SINGLE ISSUE PUBLISHED NEAREST TO FILING DATE
A. TOTAL NO. COPIES	1900	1863
B. PAID AND/OR REQUESTED CIRCULATION		
1. Sales through dealers and carriers, street vendors and counter sales	77	8
2. Mail Subscription	981	912
C. TOTAL PAID AND/OR REQUESTED CIRCULATION	1058	920
D. FREE DISTRIBUTION BY MAIL, CARRIER OR OTHER MEANS SAMPLES, COMPLIMENTARY, AND OTHER FREE COPIES	75	310
E. TOTAL DISTRIBUTION	1133	1230
F. COPIES NOT DISTRIBUTED	767	633
G. TOTAL	1900	1863

11. I certify that the statements made by me above are correct and complete

Vice President